ADVOCACY IN SOCIAL WORK
David and Toby Brandon

Theories in Social Work series
series editor: Professor David Brandon

VENTURE PRESS

Published by
VENTURE PRESS
16 Kent Street
Birmingham
B5 6RD

British Library Cataloguing-in-Publication Data
A catalogue record for this book is available from the British Library

ISBN   1 86178 051 6   (paperback)

Cover design by:
Western Arts
194 Goswell Road
London
EC1V 7DT

Printed in Great Britain

Contents

Page

List of Tables   Page

INTRODUCTION

This short book outlines some major issues in advocacy and social work and in particular some theories and beliefs involved. The authors are partisans not spectators. Our family has been involved in advocacy for more than forty years. One of us (David) was driven out of his job in homelessness for taking part in the successful TV programme 'Cathy Come Home' in the mid – sixties.

We describe the tensions between the demands of the paradoxical profession of social work and representing oppressed people, sometimes against your employers as oppressors. Advocates face great dangers. Their whistleblowing work often takes place against the background of the sound of shovels digging deep trenches. The messenger gets punished for the nature of the message. The recent Waterhouse report on the systemic abuse of children in care in north Wales is yet another horrific example of the way that the social worker, whistleblower, was suspended and later sacked and then entirely vindicated by the government inquiry. Shoot the messenger.

Our concern is that advocacy should be made increasingly lucid as a process. It has been used to describe processes, however worthwhile, like 'befriending' only tenuously connected with representation. Advocacy should be warm and friendly and certainly respectful but the central feature is not emotional (unlike counselling) but representational. The primary test is whether the process is effective not whether it is emotionally nourishing. We hope that the term will be used less elastically and that people will become more critical of the whole advocacy process. It isn't brown bread or apples. It needs sustained intellectual criticism to increase effectiveness, so we become worthy of the great nineteenth century pioneers like John Perceval and Elizabeth Fry.

We have focused on theories rather than practice. We want to show the development of ideas that have given drive and energy to the advocacy movement. These ideas have had a great influence on the practice of contemporary social work and pose some fundamental dilemmas. There is a great danger that service professionals like social workers and nurses will be driven out of advocacy, currently and rightly one of their major roles. Such service professional advocacy is chock full of contradictions and clashes in vested interests but nevertheless crucial in protecting individuals against oppressive services and in changing mind – sets in systems. Fully independent advocates are currently so few in number and, as yet, lacking in power and influence.

1

From another direction, service mechanisms like gagging clauses and compliance policies make it even more risky for some professionals – often whistleblowers – to speak out against internal neglect and exploitation. The costs can be very considerable, involving dismissal and exclusion. Institutions and services gain increasing skills in defending themselves against what are frequently seen as hostile insiders. Any movement away from a core responsibility for advocacy in social work and other professions, where so many vulnerable clients are regularly neglected and abused, would be tragic. We hope this small book will do a little to strengthen both that role and tradition.

To end this beginning with some irony – for the social work and nursing professions that allegedly hold advocacy close to their hearts, it has received precious little attention in the hugely expanding numbers of professional texts. To echo the most used professional cliché – this is evidence of considerable ambivalence!

David and Toby Brandon

Chapter 1
ORIGINS AND INFLUENCES

There is widespread delusion that advocacy in social care is of recent origin. 'The general concept which informs the Advocacy Movement had its origin in Scandinavia in the 1950s...' (Sim & Mackay 1997 p.9). Few things are further from the truth. A pamphlet called 'The Petition of the Poor Distracted People in the House of Bedlam' published in 1620 marked one origin of formal advocacy. (Brandon 1991 p.13). John Monro, an eighteenth century Bethlem physician attacked the whipping of lunatics as 'unnecessary, cruel, and pernicious.'(Monro 1758)

John Haslam, an early 'alienist' at the same asylum published a rebuttal of the alleged lunatic James Tilly Mathews' self-advocacy in the courts during the Napoleonic Wars. Mathews claimed to be sane in seeking his discharge from Bethlem. The professional won the legal battle but lost the war – dismissed in 1816 without a pension. (Haslam 1810). The Abbe' Sicard in Paris in the 1790s involved deaf people in the French Revolution. '

> *With the spread of the sacred names of **Liberty** and **Equality**, such unfortunates need suffer oppression no more; deaf citizens must lay claim to their human rights, confident that in the new age that is dawning they can no longer be ignored.* (Ree 1999 p.181)

A few decades further on, John Bucknill, the Superintendent of the Devon County lunatic asylum sought to restore to the lunatic 'the power of self control' and protested against the dispatching of a female lunatic, naked in a cart. (Forsyth, Melling and Adair 1996 p.337). In 1827, Elizabeth Fry, the Quaker prison reformer, pleaded for an advocacy role for women visitors.

> *During the last ten years much attention has been successfully bestowed by women on the female inmates of our prisons... But a similar care is needed for our hospitals, our lunatic asylums and our workhouses... Were ladies to make a practice of regularly visiting them, a most important check would be obtained on a variety of abuses, which are far too apt to creep into the management of these establishments...* (Rose 1994 pp.134–5)

The grandfather of modern advocacy was the brilliant visionary John Perceval. When only nine his father, then Tory Prime Minister, was assassinated at the House of Commons. Years later, John became 'mentally ill' and was kept in private mental homes for many years. His 'Narrative' published in

3

two parts (1838 and 1840) was a spiritual autobiography as well as shaping formal mental health advocacy arising out of a protest against his own experiences of abuse. 'Men acted as though my body, soul and spirit were fairly given up to control, to work their mischief and folly upon.' (Perceval 1840). In the mid 1840s Perceval set up the Alleged Lunatic's Friends Society which advocated for people in the asylums and pressed the government for radical changes. 'Many persons confined as lunatics are only so because they are not understood...' (Porter 1987 p.188 and Hunter and Macalpine 1961 pp.391–5).

Over the next twenty years, the Society fought vigorously to protect the civil liberties of mental patients; check the widespread negligence in the lunatic asylums; bring to light greed and corruption; represent the poor before the courts. Their lawyers took up the cases of more than seventy 'lunatics', unable to defend themselves. They bombarded Home Secretaries with advice, petitions and proposals for legislation. Personal slander and abuse went with the campaigns. During his protest against conditions in Northampton County Asylum (which he won) the local newspaper published a letter from an asylum official accusing him of being 'mentally deranged'. 'His sympathies with the insane are of a very morbid character and his judgement to the last feeble and weak.' (Podvoll 1990 pp.54–7)

We want to describe eight major issues and perspectives that have contributed to the development of advocacy and empowerment.

- Self Help
- Welfare Rights
- Independent Living
- Legal Advocacy
- Scandals
- Anti-discrimination
- Social Model of Disability
- Social Role Valorisation.

Self help

Pioneering advocacy work developed in fits and starts but since the 1960s there has been widespread blossoming with very little financial investment. The origins of self-advocacy are lost in time but more recently they are partly an offspring of the extensive self-help movement. Among early self-help groups were the British Deaf Association and the National League of the Blind – founded in the 1890s. (Barnes 1998) They began to band together, to understand disability as a political process rather than simply as an individual tragedy.

Wilson identifies some key principles of this movement: ownership by those who have experienced the situation bringing the group together; to be valued and appreciated, warts and all; recognition of the effort it often takes to join and respect for individual choices. 'As consumer groups, in part, self-help groups also have a role in feeding back to policy makers and practitioners on what life has been like for them as clients and patients, and how things could be better.' (Wilson in Jack 1995 pp.93–4). These groups explore some essential tensions between attention to the individual's pain and distress and the need to influence the wider systems that usually magnify that suffering.

These groups based on the membership of so-called 'devalued people' frequently battle with well-established bodies like Mencap and SCOPE, important parts of the official establishment. These clashes have been largely between organisations *for* and organisations *of*

> *...policymakers (have tried) to marginalize other forms of disability organisation by giving greater encouragement and succour to organizations for disabled people, such as the Royal Association for Disablement and Rehabilitation (RADAR) and traditional charity organizations, in comparison with activist organizations of disabled people, such as the British Council of Disabled People (BCODP), whose demands are thought to be too extreme...* (Barnes, Mercer, Shakespeare 1999 p.158)

The struggle between the relatively wealthy Mencap with a skipfull of Birthday Honours and the struggling, poverty-stricken People's First advocacy groups, hanging on grimly to short-term funding illustrates this well.

Welfare rights
The Welfare Rights movement reflected early Quaker values and the United States civil rights movement. As black people experienced high levels of poverty, radical American lawyers challenged the whole machinery of social security. Organisations like the Child Poverty Action Group (CPAG) imported these ideas to the United Kingdom. In 1968 Oxfordshire County Council appointed the first Welfare Rights Officer, giving an initial legitimacy to social security advocacy. (Bateman 1995 p.12). Throughout the 1970s and 80s there was a growth of such posts as well as in self-advocacy through the Claimants Unions supporting individuals as well as campaigning for changes in systems. They honed a method of advocacy for accessing increased welfare benefits but virtually disappeared in the early 1990s, with a similar decline in community development and community action approaches.

Social workers have a long tradition of working in social security. They

> *have been closely associated with helping to resolve benefit problems,*
> *because of their own direct involvement in practical service provision*
> *for those on low incomes, their residual income maintenance powers*
> *for children and families, and the devastating effect that poverty can*
> *have on some individuals...* (Bateman 1995 p.13)

They were tackling 'unnecessary poverty'. Many people in poverty were eligible for benefits but had difficulties in getting them. They campaigned with voluntary bodies like the CPAG to improve both the general scope and level of benefits. They became an important component of the disability lobby.

Independent Living Movement

Another important ingredient was the Independent Living Movement (IL) initially developed in the late 1970s in the United States, as more and more 'patients' moved out of the institutions, 'demanding greater independence and broader social participation for disabled persons. Along with accessible housing, supporting services, and assistive devices, a greater degree of self-determination was sought as a move away from dependency.' (Brooks 1991). The IL concept provided a new perception of people with disabilities. In contrast to the more passive images of disability by the medical and reha-bilitation models, the IL concept presents the disabled person as capable of political advocacy, self-help, and consumer control of services.' (Begum 1992). This projected a more active vision of disabled individuals with an analysis of the discriminatory nature of many services. They were no longer victims but survivors with the means to battle for better conditions.

Heavily influenced by the Independent Living Movement and the Civil Rights movement, the Americans with Disabilities Act (ADA) became law in July 1990 and was a major success for the Disability Movement and its powerful collective advocacy. ADA makes it illegal to discriminate against anyone with a disability – in employment, public services, transportation, telecommunications and access (accommodation). It provided some machinery for enforcement. The most notable improvements have been in accommodation because the lack of physical access to buildings is easier to understand. It has had a considerable knock on effect through increasing the visibility of disabled people.

ADA helped increased integration especially in the access and employment areas. *USA Today* magazine commented:

Braille dots are popping up next to numbers on automatic teller machines. Phones for the deaf are being established in sports arenas. Employers are scratching questions about medical problems from application forms. From offices to movie theatres, the impact of the most sweeping piece of civil rights legislation ever enacted is being seen, heard and felt... (Scott 1994)

The British Independent Living Movement developed similar ideas and campaigned for fresh legislation. It differed from the American tradition in that it was much more controlled by people with disabilities themselves and not by academics and other professionals. The formation of the British Council of Organisations of Disabled People (BCODP) in 1981 provided a national forum for bringing together ideas. (Liberty 1994). Consciousness raising was a key objective. People with disabilities had largely internalised the negative values of mainstream society and needed to find ways of valuing themselves in a largely hostile world.

Disabled people as a collective force have, through the disability rights movement, used the experiences and understanding of disability as social oppression to: (a) challenge the professional and public perceptions of disability as being a natural consequence of a biological condition; and (b) demand the right to self-determination and full and equal participation in the social, economic and political sphere. (Morris 1993)

This was part of a huge shift from the socially conditioned passive gratitude to assertive and even aggressive action that met with resistance from many service professionals. TV news scenes of people in wheelchairs chained to railings near Downing Street in London and even covered in red paint were graphic. There was a rejection of a caring ethos, some even seeing it as central to disempowerment. 'One cannot, therefore, have care and empowerment, for it is the ideology and the practice of caring which has led to the perception of disabled people as powerless.' (Morris 1997 p.54)

Legal advocacy

Larry Gostin and Tony Smyth developed the National Association for Mental Health, later called MIND, as a campaigning body, using legal advocacy as one prong of an attack on oppressive forces in the early 1970s. They took a series of cases mainly from the special hospital system, through the British courts and onto the European Human Rights court to establish and clarify principles of psychiatric treatment and bring the whole rights approach to the mental health system. Much of their influence is seen in the rights based 1983 Mental Health Act, especially with the introduction of the Mental Health Act Commissioners.

The Disabled Persons (Services, Consultation and Representation) Act went onto the statute book in 1986 and was another part of this push to establish both rights and advocacy and was to some extent a pyrrhic victory. 'In this Act "authorised representative", in relation to a disabled person, means a person appointed by or on behalf of that disabled person to act as his authorised representative for the purposes of this Act.' It gave people with a disability – rights to representation, to assessment, to information and to consultation. (Bingley and Hurst 1987). Over the next few years, it was mostly placed in cold storage by a Conservative government viewing it as unnecessary and expensive. (Holland 1991)

The Conservative government had difficulty with structural obligations and stressed:

> *individual rather than collective rights; rights conferring negative freedoms from restraints upon liberty, rather than positive freedoms to fulfil human potentiality; and rights calling for legal restraints upon the power of the state, rather than positive action which might change the odds under which different social groups compete.* (Donnison 1991)

The services were fundamentally based on perceptions of 'assessed need' rather than on rights and entitlements.

The campaign for legislation really caught alight in June 1994 with 2000 people lobbying Parliament during an unsuccessful attempt to get the Civil Rights (Disabled Persons) Bill through. It was eventually 'talked out' by government backbenchers. It tried to define disability and discrimination; to describe what activities would be covered by law and how they would be enforced. The government, whilst welcoming the basic principles, argued that it was prohibitively expensive – according to last minute estimates – £17 billion. Nicholas Scott, then Minister for the Disabled said: 'Comprehensive anti-discrimination legislation would present practical difficulties, lead to increased litigation and unquantifiable costs for business and taxpayers.' (*Professional Social Work* 1994 pp.8–9)

Perhaps the most crucial and eventual result of this powerful campaign was the Disability Discrimination Act, taking effect at the end of 1996, an attempt to bite on the problems of marginalisation, exclusion and poverty. It gave the UK's 2.2 million disabled people of working age, the right not to be discriminated against 'unjustifiably', gives employers a duty to make 'reasonable' adjustments to the workplace to accommodate them.

The Disability Lobby complained that it was all too vague and contained few real sanctions. The Disability Rights Commission established in 2000 is one attempt to deal with those reservations. This Commission has powers to formally investigate cases, as well as provide central information and advice to disabled people, business, employers and service providers. It also has responsibilities for research and to advise Government. It sees not only the legal framework but also the whole social culture as obstacles to the full participation of disabled people in society. (Sayce and Bates 2001 pp.8–9)

There were also some successes in childcare. The 1989 Children Act introduced a new category of children in need, specifically including disabled children and re-defined an advocacy figure – the guardian ad litem.

For the first time, disabled children were specifically included in children's legislation, integrated with other groups of children, rather than being included, almost by default, in legislation designed with adults in mind.

A child is disabled if he is blind, deaf or dumb or suffers from mental disorder of any kind or is substantially and permanently handicapped by illness, injury or congenital deformity or such disability as may be prescribed. (Middleton 1992)

Formal advocacy for children and young people began in 1987 with the appointment of children's rights officers by some local authorities; the first in Leicestershire.

Scandals

Large numbers of scandals in the 1960s and 1970s had a great influence on the shape of community care policy. For example the Ely Mental Handicap Hospital (1969) inquiry in Cardiff found that numbers of patients were treated cruelly and neglectfully and kept in appalling conditions. Children's advocacy flourished partly from numbers of well-publicised court cases, concerning the abuse of children. Regular scandals from the Maria Colwell case (killed at six years old by her step-father in 1973) onwards and many reporting terrible conditions in psychiatric and mental handicap hospitals were a major influence on the shape of policies. These scandals and their enquiries rediscovered child abuse and negligent and abusing systems. This inspired overtly political and legal activity. The law was used as a weapon to promote radical change. 'Organisations such as the Children's Legal Centre, the National Children's Bureau and the Family Rights Group all sought to use legal solutions on behalf of those involved in care disputes.' (Hayden, Goddard, Gorin and van der Spek 1999 p.26)

"Children at special school forced to eat vomit"
*Children at a council run special school were forced to swallow their own vomit, an inquiry heard yesterday. If any parents complained...
their children were denied treats such as horse riding and swimming...*
(The Guardian, 4 February 1992)

Another example of wholesale institutional abuse came from the Staffordshire 'Pindown' inquiry. Pindown involved 'solitary confinement and behaviour control, but was essentially a degrading and humiliating treatment forced upon children. For example, children were isolated in confinement rooms, where they were made to wear night clothes, and copy out telephone directories...' (Westcott and Cross 1996 p.72). This and many other 'scandals' gave direction and energy to representation.

The social work profession, charged with the protection of children, must find itself a moral centre, allow its members the right to be responsible for their actions, and face the great dilemma of members policing each other as well as its clients, and of discharging that responsibility in an honourable manner.' (Taylor in Hunt 1998 chapter 2)

We are a very long way off from those fine words.

One measure of how very far off, comes from the recently published Waterhouse enquiry into physical and sexual abuse in child care establishments in north Wales. This investigation covered more than 40 homes and found extensive bullying, gross sexual abuse as well as extensive emotional and mental abuse. *The Guardian* editorial commented: 'There was a familiar pattern to the start of the scandal; a whistleblower (Alison Taylor – a social worker) who was not only not believed, but suspended and later sacked.' (The Guardian, 16 February, 2000). The great majority of her allegations were vindicated in the final report but the price paid was extremely high.

Anti-discrimination
The powerful idea that the United Kingdom was divided sharply along race and gender lines has a legacy in the growth of social legislation of the sixties and seventies. The Sex Discrimination Act (1975) and the Race Relations Act (1976) reflected a great deal of dissatisfaction with an unequal society. Both Acts recognised the various hurdles to full participation that women and people from ethnic minorities faced and tried to introduce relevant remedies. They were particularly concerned with employment practices that discriminated against women and black people, and resulted in high proportions of unemployed or, if working, receiving lower wages.

Women during the 1980s have been differentially affected by poverty when compared with men, and constitute the majority in almost identical proportions to the number of women in poverty at the turn of the century. This would indicate that the welfare state has had little impact on the position of women as recipients of benefits. (Denney 1998 p.118)

By 1990 the rate of unemployment for Afro-Caribbeans, Pakistanis and Bangladeshis was double the rate for white people. (Ibid p.103). RRA 1976, for example, made it illegal to discriminate directly in areas of employment, housing and in the provision of goods and services to the public.

More specifically, personal social services gradually awoke to their internal problems, that they reflected these inequalities. For example, although women constituted a large majority of workers, very few found their way in to upper management. Black people often experienced insensitivity and active hostility to their cultural differences but also found themselves at the wrong end of the controlling aspects of social services. High proportions, especially of Afro-Caribbeans, were admitted compulsorily to mental hospitals; large percentages of black children taken into care. (Parrott 1999)

The battle in disability was increasingly against discrimination – everything from lack of access for wheelchairs to cinemas; to transport problems and employment issues. This struggle took place against a background of international declarations. For example, the United Nations Declaration on the Rights of Mentally Retarded Persons defined the rights to personal advocacy, to protection from abuse and degrading treatment and to proper legal safeguards against any unwarranted restriction of rights. (United Nations 1971). These declarations were all the more remarkable because their demands were so banal.

Table 1.1
People's first self advocacy group for people with learning difficulties

- 'the right to ask for what we want, realising that others have the right to say no
- the right to have an opinion, feeling and emotions and to express them appropriately
- the right to make statements which have no logical basis and which we do not have to justify
- the right to make our own decisions and to cope with the consequences
- the right to choose whether or not to get involved in the problems of someone else
- the right not to know about something and not to understand the right to make mistakes
- the right to privacy.'

(Lancs Advocacy Development 1993)

Initially fine words like these meant little to the everyday lives of disabled individuals. Across the world, people with disabilities were oppressed with few rights and little redress.

> *Psychiatric patients lose the right to vote in Japan, India and, in some instances, in Britain and the USA. In Holland, Egypt and many European countries, they lose the right to administer their own property. In Japan, Egypt and Israel they lose the right to write and receive uncensored mail. In most countries, outside America, patients do not have the right to refuse treatment.* (Cohen 1988 p.30)

Campaigners protested vigorously against an ocean of oppression swept by huge waves of pity, compassion and welfare.

> *Not only has state welfare failed to ensure the basic human rights of disabled people, but it has also infringed and diminished some of these rights. It has done this, for example, by providing segregated residential facilities which deny some disabled people the right to live where they choose, and by imposing assessment procedures which deny some disabled people the right to privacy.'* (Rogers and Pilgrim 1993)

They were heavily influenced by struggles against racism and sexism. 'Disability is a human rights issue requiring political action rather than a social problem requiring welfare provision.' (Oliver 1993)

Those barriers are particularly prevalent in employment. SCOPE summarises as in the table below:

Table 1.2   Disabling employment barriers

• More likely to be long-term unemployed
• More than a third of 2.2 million disabled people want to work, only 5% annually come off state benefits to start jobs
• Six times more likely to face discrimination on applying for work than able-bodied people
• Work gained by disabled people likely to be poorly paid and low-skilled.
• 62% of those seeking work felt they had been refused a job or interview because of their disability
• 35% of disabled people had been unable to accept a job because the building housing it was inaccessible.
(The Observer 20 February:2000, p.16)

Social model of disability

An influential mix of academics (mostly disabled themselves) and disabled people constructed the social model of disability, drawing again on North American influences, putting it in the whole context of a struggle against an overwhelmingly oppressive society. This tried to take power back especially from medical professionals and redefine the issues in terms of the everyday experiences, often highly negative, of people with disabilities.

> *Disabled people are in the process of liberating themselves from another force, which has constrained them for centuries: the medical profession. Doctors and paramedics colonized disability, and turned it into material for research and experimentation.* (Baird in Oliver 1996, p.121)

For example, one seminal battle has been about turning the description of a group of disabled people from that of 'mentally handicapped' to 'learning difficulties' – hugely preferred by the user organisation 'People First'. Currently we have reached the unsatisfactory compromise of 'learning disabilities'.

Hemmings spells out what the social model involves:

Table 1.3   Key points of the social model

- Developed by disabled people to describe and take action against discrimination
- Developed to frame the problem of disability in social terms rather than viewing the disabled person as the problem
- Enables us to define specific areas for change, and in particular to identify negative attitudes, communication barriers and physical access as major area for improvement.
- Enables all disabled people to join together to campaign for better attitudes and improved communication and access, no matter what their impairment
- Enables disabled people to express their situation in terms of human rights, as an issue of equality
- Takes the focus away from what disabled people can't do, and puts it on what we would all do, in alliance, to bring about this equality.

                                                                    (Hemmings in Morris 1997 p.19)

This model looked squarely at the widespread evidence of both direct and indirect oppression and discrimination against disabled people and especially at the reluctance of social structures to deal with its fundamental social and economic causes. They face tremendous barriers in housing, leisure, education and transport. Under the medical and individual models, this minority was perceived as:

> *"unfortunate", useless, different, oppressed and sick...unable to "enjoy" the social and material benefits of modern living. These include the opportunity for marriage, parenthood, social status, independence and freedom, employment...* (Hunt in Barnes, Mercer and Shakespeare 1999 p.77)

There was a wholesale rejection of the notion that unfortunate personal circumstances held disabled people back – the personal tragedy perspective. This model saw the professionals and the 'disability industry' specialising in 'special needs provision' as a huge and damaging impediment. It perceived the different and often competing professions struggling to establish certain forms of hegemony over those with a disability, to turn them in to a cash crop. Huge voluntary bodies 'serving' those with disabilities had little representation on their major policy making committees of those allegedly served.

The greatest 'symptoms' of disability were perceived as poverty and exclusion. 'Mental health problems disrupt and reduce personal income and resources because those subject to it find themselves disadvantaged in sustaining employment. This disadvantage is not just a question of clinical condition disrupting an individual's capacity for work, it is also a reflection of the attitudes to mental health difficulties which prevail in wider society.' (Davis and Wainwright 1996 p.47). There is little real evidence, beyond political rhetoric, of any serious attempts to socially and economically include large numbers of marginalised people.

Social role valorisation

In the early 1980s, the principle of normalisation, later renamed social role valorisation (SRV) became extremely influential, especially in learning disability circles and to a lesser extent in mental health. Wolf Wolfensberger, the North American academic who did much to shape its meaning, provided the brief definition 'The use of culturally valued means in order to enable people to live culturally valued lives.' (Brandon 1988)

Wolfensberger's view was that the health and social services largely contributed to the essentially devalued status of a wide variety of their 'clients'. Through congregating and segregating processes on which their services were fundamentally based, they magnified the stigma of socially and economically marginalised people like the elderly, the disabled... These apartheid services, largely unintentionally, excluded them from accessing mainstream facilities like libraries, cinemas, theatres and especially employment.

Wolfensberger outlined seven core themes underpinning this destructive process.

Table1.4   SVR Core themes

Unconsciousness: largely unexamined processes leading to increases in the fundamental devaluing of persons perceived as negatively different, strongly influencing the health and social services provision
Role expectations: holding low expectations of service users, minimising their potential and assigning them lives which contain poverty in a materialistic and spiritual sense
Deviancy magnification: crowding devalued individuals together multiplies the perceived stigma by the public
Personal competence: services need belief in people's abilities to achieve – realistic optimism. This emphasises achievement rather than handicap
Imitation: users are offered poor models to copy; they need valued ways of living like becoming tenants, lovers, parents, workers...
Imagery: service imagery is often negative and strange; it should enhance the value of those using it rather than exploit the pathetic aspects.
Social integration: users need access to buildings; respect from those who work with them; opportunity for a satisfying private life; full citizenship; living in a society that actively encourages inclusion on all levels. <div align="right">(Brandon 1988)</div>

SRV is centrally concerned about model coherence. Did the experience of service users equal the intentions of planners and managers? Goffman had earlier expressed this great tension even better than the SRV theorists.

> *Many total institutions, most of the time, seem to function merely as storage dumps for inmates, but...they usually present themselves to the public as rational organisations designed consciously, through and through, as effective machines for producing a few officially avowed and officially approved ends. It was also suggested that one frequent official objective is the reformation of inmates in the direction of some ideal standard. This contradiction, between what the institution does and what officials must say it does, forms the basic context of the staff's daily activity.* (Goffman 1961)

People came to these 'dumps' and either died inside or emerged more socially devalued than before.

Organisational cultures

SRV can be considered a useful tool for examining the structure of services. The 'PASS' (Programme Analysis of Service Systems) courses offered a comprehensive checklist to service design and evaluation, however as a conceptual framework it was rather limited. No examination of the relationships between organisational structure and the informal hierarchies and networks of day to day practice that govern services is made. Much needed is a conceptual framework for analysing organisations more sensitively to these issues. The theory of 'service forums' (Brandon, 1999) provides a socio-organisational analysis of services. In doing so it illuminates the disparity between official stances held by organisations and the day to day practices experienced by the disabled service users.

This book points out two neglected aspects of advocacy work. Firstly not only should advocacy be concerned with individual or group representation but it must also effect a change at an organisational and/or policy level. Secondly it should challenge the culture of organisations born out of the day to day practices of professionals.

The service forum encapsulates the routines and regimes, both official and unofficial, which transmit and block power. These forums subdivide into 'service postures' and 'service cultures'. Neither cultures or postures exist in isolation, but feed off one another. Mondros *et al* (1994) importantly note that power within organisations does not necessarily come from formal hierarchies and it is not synonymous with authority. Power therefore can be transmitted or blocked through informal and unofficial routes.

The forum of any organisation is both its government in terms of 'top floor bureaucracy' and its personality in terms of 'street level bureaucracy'. Its posture is relatively fixed and may include current welfare policy, funding objectives, political trends and the intentions of professional bodies in sets of values and beliefs. This may also include the organisation's rubric or philosophical objectives, that is the inherent, internal and formal stances taken. It is an official set of responses and fixed purposes, more reactive and passive than the active and proactive nature of the culture. The culture of an organisation has more scope for change and may contain elements of personal interest, local public opposition and daily working pressures. The service culture is therefore the unofficial presentation of the organisation through its everyday contact. It may emanate from the service posture, it can be complementary, in opposition or quite separate to it.

Lipsky's (1980) analysis of 'street-level bureaucracies' provided important clues about this culture. He explains how workers influence policy: 'public policy is not best understood as made in legislatures or top-floor suites of high-ranking administrators, because in important ways it is made in the crowded offices and daily encounters of street-level workers.' (p.24). Street-level bureaucrats like any care workers are torn between service users' requests for more and better services and policy makers' demands for efficient and effective resource management. Workers use many mechanisms for creating routines to cope with these pressures. One method is to distance themselves from service users and inflict punitive action on those behaving in 'inappropriate' ways. People may quite readily be given a 'difficult client' label from a professional. Lipsky describes these actions as 'agency behaviour', an important part of organisational culture.

When a service has a forum where posture and culture are well aligned, they have 'service forum coherency', meaning that an organisation's official objectives and rubric (often in the policy documents) are close to unofficial working practices (recorded through interviews and observed first hand). If there is a clear disparity between posture and culture then it has 'service forum incoherency'. Billis (1984 p.1) writes on welfare bureaucracies:

> *What I found striking – and the reason for the biographical aside – was the void that existed in many settings between the grand statement of general intent (ideologies, theories, and the like) and life at the institutional grassroots.*

The tensions between postures and cultures pull staff in different directions, the strong institutionalising culture of some organisations can soon mould new staff into disrespectful working practices. The culture of an organisation needs to be exposed to challenge these stigmatising processes.

Dangers for advocacy
In this great tide towards user involvement in service provision, there are immense dangers. One major problem lies in the drift towards the 'dictatorship of the articulate'. We must use advocacy to forward the interests not only of the vigorous and mouthy but also of those who are extremely vulnerable and usually forgotten, even by the Disability Movement itself. Many people have no voice, literally as well as politically – patients on psychiatric back wards, those with dementia, many homeless people... As Burton suggests – it is farcical to expect, at least in the short term, that these people could become 'active citizens' Burton (1997).

Another problem is that the Disability Movement echoes some of the exclusive features of mainstream society, sometimes referred to as 'wheelchairism'.

> *Those of us who appear not to fit in with the established and received order are inevitably ostracised and marginalised. Such has been the fate of Black Disabled people in Britain. We have been isolated and excluded not only from mainstream society, but also from the Black rights movement and the predominantly white, wider Disability Movement as well. The sum of all their experiences has been to render Black Disabled people invisible both within and without their communities.* (Stuart 1992)

There has also been a considerable struggle for mental health survivors and those with learning difficulties to become fully involved and accepted within the Movement.

But perhaps the greatest and injurious temptation lies in 'success'. The Advocacy Movement could become co-opted; a part of the oppressive systems that is should be combating. A tiny and fragile movement relying on largely short-term funding from 'tainted' sources like social services departments and health authorities could very easily get gobbled up or seduced. As we shall see later in this book, there are already considerable signs of that happening – advocates becoming valued team members, valued but not by us.

The New Zealand mental health survivor, Mary O'Hagan, comments of her contact with the survivor groups and their links with our professionals and official bodies. 'Because the British are more concerned with reforming the system they have a lot more contact with professionals. It is common for groups of survivors to admit professionals to their membership as 'allies'. In some groups the professionals have taken over; in other groups the survivors say they are happy with the professionals' involvement.' (O'Hagan 1993 p.73)

> *Co-optation or mimicking the conventional services is the most insidious and disturbing development in today's survivor movement and it needs to be faced up to. If self-help is supposed to return power and competence to survivors this must be reflected in our alternatives. How can we be sure that consumer run services don't degenerate to the level of the conventional services?* (Ibid p.93)

She is right to see these dangers. There is growing evidence that radical ideas coming from the ordinary everyday experiences of oppressed peoples are being McDonaldised. 'Success' in influencing government and local author-ities, sitting on a huge number of boring and largely ineffective committees, contains inherent the dangers of reformism. Discussions with powerful others in central and local government and health trusts and authorities don't necessarily bring about really fundamental changes in services driven by all sorts of powerful and covert vested interests. Advocacy and Userism can become just fashionable brand names, largely for use in glossy brochures, so that services can look progressive.

Chapter 2
WHAT IS ADVOCACY?

What exactly does advocacy mean? It is clear that people are using the term in a wide variety of ways and it has many different parental influences. We've learned about the widespread confusions. There is a considerable danger that advocacy becomes yet just another aerosol word like 'community' or 'empowerment' which is promisingly sprayed over everything but meaning hardly anything. POhWER, an advocacy organisation, suggests that, 'advocacy is not self explanatory and can mean many different things to different people.' (in Atkinson 1999, p.15)

Simons comments: 'Advocacy' is a fashionable word, often used as a sort of shorthand for worthy sentiments without much thought as to what it means.' (Simons 1993, p.4) Wolfensberger notes

> *the tremendous confusion surrounding the definition of the term... Today it is possible to find almost anything labelled advocacy, including some highly traditional and even highly dehumanizing services. Thus, placing a person in an institution might very well be called 'case work advocacy' or 'counselling advocacy' ... In fact, this bandwagon phenomenon has almost the effect of perverting and undermining a genuine advocacy approach and I have personally called it 'Kraft cheese advocacy', in analogy to the Kraft cheese adverts that in essence propose that one should take any kind of food and add cheese to it. Today, people would like to continue what they have always done, but add the word advocacy to it.* (Wolfensberger 1977 p.18)

Atkinson argues that advocacy is: 'A way to defend the interests of a person, and to make sure their needs are met especially someone who already feels disempowered.' (Atkinson 1999 p.16). Wolfensberger outlines three elements: 'vigor and vehemence' by which he means an essential passion and depth of feeling. He suggests further that the process must involve sacrifice, otherwise it is 'no more than Kraft cheese advocacy'. It must be 'maximally free of conflict of interest.' (Wolfensberger 1977 pp.19–20). This is a typically grim Wolfensberger posture – the Kamikazi approach, extremely low on fun and enjoyment. He doesn't bring in measures of effectiveness. Personally we'd prefer the O.J. Simpson legal team if pushed. They were all ego-maniacs without any sign of troublesome ethics but they would get you off!

19

Davies describes the context of advocacy in his influential social work textbook. 'Strategies of change in social work might sometimes need to be directed, not at the client, but at dysfunctional elements in the client's environment.' He makes a distinction between personal and structural advocacy.

In either case, the assumption is that the social worker has skills and qualities or access to resources that are likely to tip the balance in the favour of those whose interests would otherwise be overlooked or over-ridden. (Davies 1994)

Here we see again the extension of psycho-pathological terminology, in this case the ugly 'dysfunctional', used a great deal in individual work, to apply to systems and environments.

We have tried to offer a more precise definition:

Advocacy involves a person(s), either a vulnerable individual or group or their agreed representative, effectively pressing their case with influential others, about situations which either affect them directly or, and more usually, trying to prevent proposed changes which will leave them worse off. Both the intent and the outcome of such advocacy should increase the individual's sense of power; help them to feel more confident, to become more assertive and gain increased choices. (Brandon 1995 p.1)

This places the emphasis on instrumental elements without denying the importance of expressive elements. Advocacy should involve a warm and respectful process but the main ingredient lies in *the accomplishment of tasks defined by the client*. It also recognises that advocacy has been largely reactive so far. 'Shutting the stable door after the horse has bolted.' The process has been more concerned with crises and fire fighting rather than in constructing systems that prevent the horse from bolting.

Atkinson describes four key principles underpinning advocacy detailed below (Atkinson 1999 p.12):-

Empowerment: this involves gaining and in some cases regaining the power to take decisions and make choices in all areas of life – from what to eat at breakfast to where to go on holiday. It recognises to quote that quintessential Englishman, Dr Samuel Johnson that 'the road to Hell is paved with good intentions.' Clients have frequently been oppressed 'for their own good' and even more cleverly empowerment has become a method used to reconcile people to being powerless. Our systems are extremely seductive and manipulative.

As we noted earlier, social services are traditionally disempowering. Staff behave in ways that clientise the individuals under their care. They no longer remain authentic citizens after entry to the day centres, old people's homes, psychiatric hospitals... One early text, edited by Barbara Robb on the need for advocacy in institutions outlined a wide range of abuses. Two social workers described para-military regimes and oppression in two mental hospitals.

> *By consigning the elderly, with such thoughtlessness and often with such deception, to those vast and crowded pools of helplessness which we are content to accept as their last refuges, we brand ourselves as a society which, far from honouring old age, tried to banish it completely from the mind.'* (Robb 1967 p.68)

One aspect of the struggle towards empowerment, from care to rights, lies not only in understanding the destructive nature of health and social services but analysing and rejecting the individual model of disability. This model was based on a personal tragedy idea, borrowing elements from notions of sickness.

Daily Crap

Brave Cathy struggles to overcome tragedy to gain paralympics medal

---

In great contrast the disability campaigners actively adopted a social model.

> *In our view it is society which disables physically impaired people. Disability is something imposed on top of our impairments by the way we are unnecessarily isolated and excluded from full participation in society. Disabled people are therefore an oppressed group in society.* (UPIAS 1976 p.14)

Oliver valuably distinguished between individual and social models:

> *...we are increasingly demanding acceptance from society as we are, not as society thinks we should be. It is society that has to change not individuals and this change will come about as part of a process of political empowerment of disabled people as a group and not through social policies and programmes delivered by establishment politicians and policy makers nor through individualised treatments and interventions provided by the medical and para-medical professions.* (Oliver 1996 p.37)

This presented a direct and full-frontal challenge to the sacred traditions of social casework and its suppositions of knowing what was best for people. The attention was turned strongly and disturbingly (at least to the professionals) on the oppressive structures and systems rather than on their vulnerable 'victims'.

There is an enormous debate about discrimination in this profession with little practical action. Social work debates can put just a gloss on new forms of paternalism or involve vague expressions of guilt. Our vocabulary is simply extended.

> *...there is a danger that the professions who make a living out of disability have now learned the language of the social model of disability. The rhetoric is all there about 'people with disabilities' and 'empowering' but in reality there is little evidence that attitudes and practices have significantly changed unless they are tied in to practical policies. While the rhetoric of community care, for example, is about disabled people negotiating their own care packages, decisions concerning who will be entitled to what resources are still firmly in the control of social services departments.* (Leach 1996 p.94)

The journey from rhetoric to changes in practice that impact on the everyday lives of people with disabilities is a long one. Presently it is largely restricted to the glossy pages of the impressive, coloured service brochures.

We tried to sketch out through our work with SCOPE and elsewhere – a power audit system. How could you find out whether there was a genuine process of power transfer? The central feature for us was how staff were appointed. If the service users were genuinely involved in all levels of appointments, the litmus paper test showed the service had serious ambitions for empowerment – the transfer of power from staff to clients.

Table 2.1   Power audit

> *Improving information systems*
> How people got to know...? What could the various stakeholders – staff, relatives, users... easily find out? Could users read their casefiles? Could both the staff and users find out about the policy decisions made by the organisation?
>
> *Increasing consultation*
> How seriously did the service take user/staff feedback? Was there an absence of defensiveness? Could the service easily react and make the necessary changes?
>
> ▶

◀

Developing advocacy
What external restrictions were there on the possible misuses of power? If complaints were not dealt with to the satisfaction of the resident, were independent people called in?

Expanding democratic methods
How equal in power were the various people at all levels? Could residents influence management systems? Did they have a right of veto over some issues? Were users treated as full citizens?

Opting out
Could people choose some other service(s) or none? Through direct payments or some other system, could they take the money and purchase their own services and supports?

(Brandon 1991)

In social work, anti-oppressive practice expressing issues of empowerment grow in influence. Dominelli defined it as:

> *a form of social work practice which addresses social divisions and structural inequalities in the work that is done with 'clients' (users) or workers. Anti-oppressive practice aims to provide more appropriate and sensitive services by responding to people's needs regardless of their social status. ...(it) embodies a person-centred philosophy, an egalitarian value system concerned with reducing the deleterious effects of structural equalities on people's lives; a methodology focusing on both process and outcome; and a way of structuring relationships between individuals that aims to empower users by reducing the negative effects of hierarchy in their immediate interaction and the work they do together.* (Dominelli 1993 p.24)

Discrimination, arising from oppressive postures, can involve direct or indirect processes. Direct discrimination occurs when someone, or a whole group is treated differently (either positively or negatively) from another, solely or mainly because they belong to a particular social category. Indirect discrimination invokes the significance of 'inbuilt patterns of inequality rather than the particular actions of individuals'. (Blakemore and Drake 1997 p.9)

All this earnest discussion and anxious heart-searching seems to go over the heads and detached from the ordinary experiences of people in the marginalised groups, whose consciousness has to be raised. We can hear our

Mother, Grandmother – muttering on returning from the Churches she cleaned vigorously – about someone on TV like Germaine Greer – 'What does she know about the way ordinary women live!?' She needed absolutely no consciousness raising.

Autonomy: to self-determine, to be seen by others as unique and to live a daily life that expresses their individual needs. From its earliest inception, social work had severe problems with this difficult concept. Felix Biestek, one of the founding fathers of the modern profession, included client self-determination as one of his seven key principles. He defines it and then hedges it about with a number of qualifications.

> *The principle of client self-determination is the practical recognition of the right and need of clients to freedom in making their own choices and decisions in the casework process. Caseworkers have a corresponding duty to respect that right, recognize that need, stimulate and help to activate that capacity for self-direction by helping the client to see and use the available and appropriate resources of the community and of his own personality. The client's right to self-determination, however, is limited by the client's capacity for positive and constructive decision making, by the framework of civil and moral law, and by the function of the agency.* (Biestek 1961 p.103)

Clients are to be given self-determination and one major aim of social casework is to support them in gaining a greater capacity to make their own decisions. However, this freedom is dependent on their 'capacity for positive and constructive decision making.' Who is to be the judge of this? Presumably the caseworker acts as overall referee. What qualifications does he or she have? We've seen this essential dilemma charging down the nineteenth and twentieth centuries, dressed in a wide number of disguises.

One major expression of empowerment is autonomy, to express the self in a wider range of ways. A dominant feature of services is their conscious and unconscious attempts to manipulate and restrict any form of self-expression. It is one of the major elements that strikes the visitor to almost any form of day or residential services. Their structures and rituals are largely unconsciously arranged to inhibit the expression of individuality – set meal times, fixed customs... 'This is the way we do things here.' The pressure is on the client to fit in to the service, to be grateful.

There is a common social work 'catch twenty two' principle as we have seen in these pages. Clients are seen as having problems for which they are, to some extent, to 'blame'. Their personal decision making is flawed, damaged or immature. Professionals are entitled, through legal mandate, 'superior' knowledge or therapeutic skills, to supervise some or all of their life. As we've noted this is the social work helicopter position, hovering over individuals with the perceived ability to see the larger picture (!). Not just an issue of knowing best but of knowing much better. This entitles us to socially engineer people's lives, to manipulate others, the lesser mortals – the exact opposite of what advocacy should mean and intend. Prue Leith, the best selling cookery writer, complained about old people being bullied in to healthy diets. 'The emphasis (in old people's homes) should be switched to the pleasure of eating, and old people should be encouraged to eat what they like, not what they should.' (in Jeremy Laurance, *The Independent*, 9 June 1999). To turn the psycho-dynamic tables around, this is not so much staff acting in Loco Parentis (one teenager translated as lunatic parent) but staff acting as an alternative alter-ego.

To change these massively restrictive and paternalistic ideologies and structures will take a lot of wisdom and energy, and as we have seen from the various social work texts, we have no cornucopia. Those destructive ideologies are deeply embedded in the inherent nature of our culture and the professional expressions of it.

Table 2.2 Services need

An overall belief in individual choices – especially the importance of making mistakes. What Robert Perske calls 'the dignity of risk' (Wolfensberger 1972).

Respect – discouragement of paternalism and emotional suffocation.

Experience – needing a wide variety of experiences to discover what they want and need; to explore positive role models like student, worker, citizen, lover, partner.

Money – choices require cash for example travelling around, going for meals, visiting pubs, holidays...

This involves a huge power transfer that takes place only with great difficulty. As we saw from the power audit, it encourages service users to make the larger decisions and often conflicts with other social work roles that contain a 'locus parentis' element. The social worker is pulled in ideologically different directions – having to take a 'good of the client stance' at the same time as being instructed by the client about what he or she wants. They also face cultures of 'risk assessment'; a major influence from the scandal enquiries that condemn them whatever they do or don't do; their other roles as state agents give them massive responsibilities for seeing usually that a number of things *don't happen* within supervised families. The pressure on them is to play it safe.

O'Sullivan identifies four levels of involvement in decision making by clients. These levels move from hardly any involvement to the client making decisions with or without assistance.

Table 2.3   Involvement levels

- Being told:given the results of decisions made by others
- Being consulted: the client's opinions are being taken into account in the decision making.
- Being a partner: decisions jointly made – the client with the professional(s)
- Being in control: the client decides with or without the facilitation of the social worker. (O'Sullivan 1999 pp.45–50)

Moody (1992) provides a critic of autonomy as the sole means to empowerment by stating that:

> *insisting upon the ideal of autonomy contradicts disturbing facts about the conditions of frail elderly men and women – above all, with the erosion of their power to choose and of the ability to carry out their choices. The irony is that we want to uphold autonomy for the elderly at just the time when their conditions make autonomy least attainable and at a time in life when other human needs – for care, for respect, for meaning – are more pressing.*

Moody (1992) here is not saying there is anything intrinsically wrong with autonomy except in its over use. To him autonomy is not synonymous with respect. The emphasis here is to consider respect for a person within the context of their personal life histories. The answer in terms of empowerment must lie in the tension between autonomy, respect, well-being and protection.

- Citizenship: to make sure that people get the rights to which they are entitled. As we've seen that has involved a powerful movement from the passive 'clienthood' to more active terms like 'citizenship', 'survivor' and sometimes 'consumer' played out against a back ground of evolving legal and service principles, some of which have not been very constructive. The citizen aspect was concerned with people having much greater say in decisions made by bodies impacting on their lives, along with participation in local and national politics. This would help them gain membership of the relevant forums influencing both local and national issues.

Centrally this means giving people greater control, especially over the things that influence their daily lives like education, housing and transport...

> *There's a feeling that the way to do it (consumer involvement) is to re-organise people. You can do it till the cows come home and nothing will change. You've got to change the culture. You've got to focus on the process of arriving at policies.* (in Beresford and Croft 1993, p.178)

Existing systems have a definite gift for adopting radical languages and remaining more or less the same, as we saw in the section on service cultures.

Voluntary organisations and statutory bodies have been reluctant to go down that road. Working in the homeless field we are struck by how few homeless people serve on the various management boards and paternalistic many of the structures are. Bahr comments sagely:

> *With the attenuation of his affiliations goes what little power the homeless man could command. The stranger, especially the aged, scarred, alcoholic, and deformed stranger, has no social margin. He may be free to come and go, subject always to the approval of the powerful affiliated ones about him. He is on the outside; their organizations and programs represent their interests, not his. The disaffiliate has no voice in their decisions about his treatment or his future.* (Bahr 1973 p.287)

In these organisations there is usually a substantial delusion that the interests of the organisation and the service users are much the same or similar. Few things could be further from the truth.

Citizenship has three strands: political, social and civil. Many people in our community are perceived or feel that they're non-citizens. They have been cast out or were never genuinely included. Marshall defined the civil element as 'the liberty of the person, freedom of speech, thought and faith, the right to own property and to conclude valid contracts and the right to justice.' (Marshall 1975). Earlier we saw the struggle that social work has had with much of that. One fundamental irony is that this profession is one of the few that are inherently stigmatising. Just by getting a visit from a social worker the individual begins to grapple with aspects of social exclusion.

- Inclusion/exclusion: services for clients have often been unnecessarily segregated and congregated, encouraging exclusion and even demonisation, as with paedophiles, militating against inclusion in ordinary valued settings like libraries, pubs and restaurants. Excluded people used 'special' and usually devalued services.

The principle of normalisation, more recently re-named Social Role Valorisation (SRV) has been at the heart of the debates about social inclusion and exclusion over the last twenty years. Wolfensberger, one of the main founders of this principle, cites four main responses to those perceived as deviant – destruction, prevented from acting deviantly, supported to have the deviant condition reversed and segregated. (Wolfensberger 1987). The health and social services were centrally involved in these processes of social rejection through interventions that involved segregation and congregation, achieving the exclusion of large numbers of people with disabilities.

For the advocate, the issue of self-oppression and exclusion raises very difficult and complicated problems. In this the service user internalises much of the perceived negative social and economic processes. We can see this sort of overall process:

- MAJOR SOCIAL AND ECONOMIC FORCES
- HAVE AS A BY-PRODUCT – **SOCIAL CASUALTIES**
- **DEVALUED** BY OTHERS: SEEN AS STRANGE, DANGEROUS, USELESS, INADEQUATE...
- USING **APARTHEID** SERVICES THAT OTHERS DON'T USE
- USERS INTERNALISE DEVALUING

Self-oppression, the internalising of the oppressive values of the powerful majority can lead to devalued people perpetuating their own oppression. Adam explores a theory of self-hatred in some of these groups, suggesting that they go through a common process of accommodation, compliance and resistance in their struggle to seek some sort of self-worth and inclusion on their own terms. (Adam 1990 pp.53–67)

Adam sees five interrelated stages in the development of an oppressed consciousness. **Mimesis** involves hiding what you really are and attempting to pass oneself off as a member of the dominant group. **Guilt expiation** involves 'being riddled with internalised self-hatred and guilt and engaging in circular, self-destructive rituals, serving to punish them, and ultimately reinforce the portrait they have of themselves as 'devalued persons' and is 'a self-negating project aimed ultimately at self-affirmation.' **Psychological withdrawal** involves 'a flight from identity and in some extreme cases a flight from reality, as when there is a psychotic break, only further isolates the individual from others sharing the same fate.' The last two stages – **Social withdrawal** and **Contraversion** involve some remedies. These involve the construction of new versions of reality on the basis of the re-appropriation of one's own historical condition.

The principal role of the social worker in helping oppressed clients (in these last two stages) is to insure that these stages are accorded their proper time and place. If workers are the least bit uncomfortable with conflict, they may find it difficult to assist oppressed clients to separate themselves from those who dominate them. They may thus prematurely encourage oppressed groups to engage in dialogue with their oppressors without their first having had the time and opportunity to define and con-solidate their own identity. (Adam in Moreau 1990)

This concept of self-hatred or self-incarceration is valuable and was expressed bluntly in a Durham childhood as 'Give the working man a whip and he'll whip himself.' One can easily see the dangers in this sort of approach. In perceiving ourselves as having a greater understanding than the oppressed, we are almost halfway towards the helicopter view taken by the therapists. 'I can see more than you.' We are in danger of not taking instruc-tions but of making interpretations, outlined earlier. We begin a potentially destructive voyage towards professional mystification and dogmatically applying stages, that has already happened in some other fields like bereave-ment. Just because someone (if not everyone including women) has an unresolved Oedipus complex doesn't mean they are wrong and not able to make perfectly 'good' decisions.

Another danger in Adams' view is that the onus is once more placed on disabled people to adjust to dominant mores, that they had little or no role in creating. Oliver puts the issues succinctly by quoting from Steve Biko, the murdered South African activist and transferring it to the disability context:

If by integration you understand a breakthrough into white society by blacks, an assimilation and acceptance of black into an already estab-lished set of norms and code of behaviour set up by whites, then YES I am against it... If on the other hand by integration you mean there shall be participation by all members of a society, catering for the full expression of the self in a freely changing society as determined by people, then I am with you.' (quoted in Oliver 1996 pp.92–3)

The genuine inclusion of marginalised people should involve the following elements.

- Ready access to the buildings where services take place, for example, through ramps.

- Receiving respect and esteem from others so that positive self-images are established and negative elements reduced.

- Having the opportunity for a satisfying private life.

- Seen as a valued citizen with legal status; having the vote, feeling influential, making an impact on your surroundings.

- Being able to use facilitating communication through technology or interpretation or translation.

- Living in a society with structures that assist and welcome all kinds of mixing and belonging.

Hall describes inclusion for a child with significant impairments.

Being a full member of an age-appropriate class in your local school/college doing the same lesson as the others with the others, and it mattering if you are not there. Also you have friends who spend time with you outside school/college plus others who care for you work hard to ensure that you are fully included in the mainstream of community life and use generic services along with other citizens.' (Hall 1997 pp.129–30)

These sound simple elements, not hard to access but they are extra-ordinarily difficult in our society.

Citizen advocacy has been closely linked with SRV, Wolf Wolfensberger being the dominant figure in both. Now renamed Advocacy Partners, it has always emphasised the expressive aspects rather than the instrumental side. It has been concerned with social inclusion rather than representation. O'Brien puts it characteristically beautifully.

A citizen advocate is a valued citizen who is unpaid and independent of human services creates a relationship with a person at risk of social exclusion and chooses one or several ways to understand and respond to, and represent that person's interests as if they were the advocate's own thus bringing their partner's gifts and concerns in to the circles of ordinary human life.' (O'Brien 1981 in Brandon *et al*, 1995 p.83)

As we've noted earlier, this particular form of advocacy has been primarily concerned with social inclusion, through the long-term support of the valued advocacy/partner. The emphasis has been mainly on the expressive process rather than the achievement of any designated instrumental tasks. Wolfensberger makes the important distinction between these two basic elements (1977).

Table 2.4

'Instrumental' tasks	'Expressive' tasks
advise and assist with everyday tasks; decision making, transport, shopping, for example	provide emotional support during stress and crisis
administer property and income	maintain sympathetic communication and interaction
represent interests vis-á-vis the law	bring fellowship to lonely and abandoned
ensure inclusion in appropriate services; training, work, education for example	share emotionally significant activities, trips and events
	exchange meaningful tokens on special occasions

These various themes provide some general framework for advocacy. Clifford defines issues concerned with **social difference**; the links **between personal and political**; the **nature of power**; **historical and geographical location**; **reflexivity/mutual involvement**. (Clifford 1995). Social differences are inevitably involved in the disparities of power between individuals and classes, between dominant and dominated groups. The major divisions are race, gender, class, sexual preference, disability and age. Advocacy is one vital way of encouraging those who are oppressed to speak out and to seek some redress, either directly or indirectly from their oppressors. Advocates assist in this pilgrimage.

The links between the personal and political are crucial. People are not independent human islands separated from the mainland but represent a whole variety of structural inequalities in their life histories. Devalued groups like ethnic minorities or older people are subject to an intricate network of oppressive ideologies that are racist and ageist. Advocacy is profoundly structural and political. It seeks to define issues in terms of who has what power, to help those who feel vulnerable and powerless to feel they can have an influence on an essentially unjust world.

Power is shaped by a huge range of social, cultural, economic and psycho-logical factors. These strongly influence people's negative and positive attitudes to social difference. It operates at a personal and structural level. Social work advocates stand between the pressures of the social and the personal. They are pulled in opposite directions by the needs of the state to 'normalise' citizens (their employers) and to exclude some others, seen as non-productive and deviant and their wishes to represent those devalued and excluded. Their overt opposition to this oppression will not go unpunished.

Historical and geographical location – people's experiences gain meaning within specific times and places. Their context is located within social history as well as within what is happening right now. Social workers have a close view of what happens in the ordinary everyday lives of people in poverty and the frequent hypocrisy of the state.

Reflexivity/mutual involvement – means the continual consideration of how values, social differences and power affect interactions between individuals. The growth of mutuality takes place within a context not only of psychology but of sociology, history, ethics and politics. (Clifford 1995). In social work, advocacy acts as an antidote against excessive pre-occupation with elements stressing pathology and individual tragedy like many aspects of counselling. For example, Oliver quotes Segal '(disabled people) take in general two years to accept any significant loss... this means that people with disabilities are often mentally about two years out of date in terms of their physical situation.' (Oliver 1996 p.135). Thanks a bunch.

Chapter 3
ADVOCACY TYPES

The last twenty years has seen a considerable diversification but there are still only three major types, which are,

- Direct representation by the aggrieved individual.
- Representation through another, either professional or amateur.
- Organising with others to influence oppressive systems.

Hodgson argues valuably that advocacy needs two dimensions for classification:

Passive	Active
Individual	Collective

He argues that children's advocacy has traditionally been passive.

> *Child-care organisations, local authority and voluntary, have considered themselves to be advocates on the basis of representing children's "best interests." Whether these agencies are also prepared to pursue advocacy of the **rights** of children is one of the most important questions currently facing them.'* (Hodgson in Dalrymple and Hough 1995 pp.123–4)

Most of us use various sorts of professionals for our representation at one time or another. One of us (David) uses an accountant to prevent the Inland Revenue taking my goods away; an architect to state my case to a planning authority about extending our former house; a solicitor to represent me in court when I was done for driving (many years ago) without due care and attention. Rather ambitiously the Book of Common Prayer asks God, in his spare time from sorting out Kosovo, to be 'our Mediator and Advocate.'

Although advocacy is an important ingredient in the roles of many different professions, the sorts of advocacy we are describing, as we have already seen, have different origins and motivations. For example, Kohnke makes a distinction between legal and nurse advocacy:

> *Briefly the role of the advocate is to inform the client and then inform him in whatever decision he makes. This type of support differs from the support provided by a lawyer. In the practice of law, the lawyer advocate actually presents the client's case and either pleads for justice or defends the client from accusation. In the nurse advocate role, however, support means that when the client makes a decision, the nurse abides by it and defends his right to make it. The role of the advocate comprises only two functions: to inform and to support.'* (Kohnke 1982 p. 2)

If only this complex process was that simple!

Advocacy types

- Self
- Peer
- Family
- Collective
- Advocacy partners
- Service professionals
- Professional

- Self advocacy: the fundamental advocacy method involves representation by the aggrieved people themselves. It should be the ultimate goal and preferred practice for all the other forms, but anyone who has ever tried to consult a solicitor knows how difficult it is to give any instructions to a professional. We even have monthly struggles with our hairdressers!

  Self advocacy is a major means of empowering oppressed individuals so they can have an effective voice. It is one significant method in helping to redress the imbalance of power between powerful systems and exploited individuals. Dowson identifies four different themes in the field of learning difficulties.

- Self-advocacy as a **very specific and individual act**. A person assumed to have no voice, or nothing to say, speaks; and so challenges the identity they have been assigned.

- Self-advocacy as **one component of some more general activity**. Thus a case review or individual plan meeting might involve (and indeed should involve) self-advocacy as one part of a process which also includes information-sharing, decision making, and service allocation.

- Self-advocacy **as a group activity**, in which the members represent themselves and their immediate peers; some users of an adult training centre, for example, who meet to discuss issues of special concern to those who attend the centre.

- Self-advocacy as **campaigning for people with learning difficulties as a whole**. (Dowson 1991)

That is an extremely confusing ragbag of differing processes and objectives. It is to be used to cover individual and personal representation; a group activity involving self help; lobbying collectively for general changes in systems... This asks far too much of any single term and adds to the general confusion between individual, group and collective activities.

Sometimes competing forms of indirect representation, speaking on behalf of, may actively hinder this fundamental process of direct representation. The desire to rescue others, even when they're unwilling, is a powerful element in advocacy. Projecting our own wishes on to distressed others can often be almost irresistible.

Vulnerable individuals may become intentionally or even unintentionally oppressed and patronised by so-called advocates. Other forms may suppress or repress the desirable drive of 'speaking for ourselves' and develop ever more sophisticated patterns of dependency and oppression. In reality, some sorts of clients present extremely complex difficulties – those unable to speak for themselves, some of the dying; those with Alzheimer's Syndrome; those in a coma...? In what ways can self-advocacy be made relevant to their situation? How can we involve them in an empowering process, in which they can truly comprehend and participate?

Winslade *et al.,* comment.

> *It is difficult to know what should guide the substitute decision-maker. Paternalism and advocacy are two rival principles that compete as criteria for decision. If advocacy is the appropriate principle, substitute decision-makers should render a decision that they believe the patients would have chosen for themselves if they were competent. If on the other hand, paternalism is the appropriate principle, should the substitute decision-makers' own beliefs about what is in the patients' best interests determine the decision?'* (Winslade *et al.,* 1984 p. 208)

Polden raises some issues about those with dementia and criticises the Kantian social work principle of 'respect for persons.' '(It) falls short of giving a full account of the complex nature of social work intervention in relation to elderly persons who have dementia.' She suggests that the concept of 'constructive consent' is preferable. This means 'constructing' what the person would have decided if they were able to. '...the decision to give consent is based on the knowledge that the individual concerned would certainly have consented if competent to do so.' (Polden 1989 p.173–81)

This is a very seductive but immensely difficult and even potentially dangerous posture. How is anyone to understand the term 'certainly'. What if – and in all probability there will be – substantial disagreements between relatives and friends? Who is to mediate? There are obvious distinctions between people who have a before and after and those who have not. A person with a serious head injury or with Alzheimers Syndrome had a before and now has an after. A person born with multi-impairments has not – so there is no base-line to be constructed.

There are also difficult issues in self-advocacy about the instrumental elements. Advocacy should 'win', whatever that may mean for the aggrieved individuals. What if the aims, strategies and skills of the client have poor results? It may be that he or she seeks advice, gets good quality suggestions that stand an excellent chance of gaining redress and ignores it all. We've had clients who seem to throw away their opportunities for getting what they wanted. For any advocate that is immensely frustrating and it's tempting to go in to 'I told you so' mode. The whole aim of the process is to empower, even to make major mistakes. Our task in supporting is to give the best advice and suggestions we can and encourage their own decisions. We've all made so many mistakes in our lives, we're just not in any position to feel superior!

Central to this vision of this form of advocacy is *empowerment*. The aggrieved person is supported to speak out and express their complaints and demands, not someone else's or to please the advocate. This is seen as part of an overall and ongoing struggle to remedy the whole situation of all disadvantaged people – those with a disability; from ethnic minorities; in poverty; the elderly...

- Advocacy partners: a fresh name for 'citizen advocacy' although the former name is still used by many local organisations. These people 'get to know the partner by visiting, spending time together and sharing interests; speak to the right people about the partner's needs and concerns; help the partner deal with letters and forms; help the partner choose hobbies, entertainment, education or whatever he or she wants to do. (Advocacy Partners in Brandon 1995, ch 6)

'A citizen advocate is defined as a private, unpaid citizen who has developed a relationship with someone at risk of exclusion or isolation. The role of the advocate is to be "on the side" of the partner.' (Simons 1993 p. 23). Here the emphasis is on inclusion and exclusion and on the involvement of the volunteer advocate who is preferably a 'valued citizen'. The stress is usually on the expressive elements rather than on the instrumental. On the continuum going from advocacy to counselling, it can get closer to informal counselling than representation. We can hear the echoes of the founder of this sort of advocacy – Wolf Wolfensberger and the emphasis on re-valuing people who have been socially marginalised.

One danger of this sort of representation, is that the focus is primarily on the relationship between two individuals – the volunteer advocate and his or her protégé, that may have little spin off for challenging and actually changing oppressive systems. Ramcharan suggests this is the role of other representation systems, a highly unsatisfactory response. (Ramcharan in Jack 1995 pp. 237–8). In a society where advocacy is very sparsely distributed where are these other systems? You can hardly deal with inadequacies in a particular advocacy approach by referring clients to non-existent services.

Although this form of advocacy is often high on integration, helping excluded people to become part of the community, it may be low on representation. Advocates can spend a lot of time in pizza restaurants and at football grounds and not much at social security tribunals or housing benefit offices. (Brandon 1995 ch 6)

Bateman rightly sees this as a 'fundamental weakness'.

The model involves the advocate acting in a variety of roles, and the different skills needed for such roles are poorly defined. By expecting a citizen advocate to be a friend, counsellor, legal adviser and general dogsbody, too much is placed on the shoulders of most people. This, allied to the long-term commitment required, means that Citizen Advocacy is hard to sustain and harder to focus on the issues that matter to a service user. (Bateman 1995 p. 9)

It is also easy for the advocate to get sucked in to becoming part of service delivery, just another team player seeking what is best for the client, antagonistic to the whole advocacy process.

- Peer advocacy: this is where a peer, a person who is or has been in a similar situation to the client, helps represent him or her. John Perceval, mentioned earlier, was an excellent example. This type of advocate is or was an insider, for example, a mental health survivor who has been through the psychiatric system, representing a peer against an attempt to compulsorily admit to mental hospital. (Brandon in Jack 1995). This kind of advocate can act not only as an effective representative but can also serve as a positive role model. He or she has a direct experience of how the system really works and how it is possible to survive and has become a 'success.' This sort of involvement is also a way of valuing, what has mainly been perceived as a negative experience.

An advocate, himself disabled, working at the National Spinal Injuries Centre in Stoke Mandeville Hospital, is an Independent Living Advisor. His task is to advocate on behalf of clients with spinal code injury and tetraplegia to enable them to organise their own independent living schemes, using personal assistance support in pursuit of their own self-defined aims. (Morris 1993)

The dangers are that this type of advocate can very easily over-identify with the particular client. Just because I've tried to commit suicide, doesn't mean that I know how that feels for you or anyone else. It requires a considerable discipline to stay out of the excesses of the drive to rescue when the situation hits you right in the heart of your own autobiography.

Peer advocates can easily get re-clientised. Related professionals, especially those who knew them directly as clients, can perceive them not as advocates but as people needing 'help.'. Existing advocacy services are rarely able to offer adequate support and nutrition to those under attack from the twin stresses of the task and reclientisation.

The peer advocate has some sense of the internality of the social and economic issues affecting the client. He or she knows in their own ways, how some of the social context 'felt.' Those feelings, for example, like having been in care or served time in prison, may feel very different to the client, hence the dangers in over- identification by the advocate. Some of the most oppressive managers of services known to us, have been former service users.

Peers may have absolutely no talent for either support or representation. Just because they are former prisoners, have HIV or cerebral palsy – share a common disempowering experience with the client – doesn't mean they have any gifts at all in representation, negotiation or getting relevant information. They can have all the heart and feeling in the world but no talent for making out a case or lucidly communicating to powerful people and systems what the needs of the clients are, which is what he or she needs.

- *Advocacy by service professionals*: the roles of social workers and psychologists throw up some fascinating dilemmas for advocacy because they usually have so many conflicts. What about the whistleblowers, often reviled by the services they seek to change? They face strong reactions, sometimes dismissal, sending to Coventry, passed over for promotion... Can service professionals have any advocacy role without being destructive? *As this small book is primarily concerned with this form of advocacy, this section is very brief.*

- Family advocacy: families have been and are a primary support for disabled people, mostly the female members – mothers and daughters. However there are no free lunches and they are a source of some suffering as well as liberation. The Hollywood film 'Lorenzo's Oil', the story of parents battling to find a cure for their mysteriously sick son, graphically illustrates those complexities, as well as the tricky relationship with concerned professionals. Service users and their parents and children may often have very different agendas but it is clear that this type is currently by far the pre-dominant form of representation. (S. Brandon 1997)

Set up in January 1985, the Parents Involved Network Project (PIN) in Pennsylvania, USA, recruits and serves parents of children diagnosed as having serious emotional disturbances. It started as a self-help group and later developed into case advocacy for parents, looking at the needs of children with mental health problems.

Parents struggle to become their child's advocate – often learning how to make the systems respond to their needs by a trial-and-error process. More often than not, parents whose children have serious emotional problems are still looked upon as having caused their child's problems rather than as being the most important resource for their child. Many parents become overwhelmed, frustrated and emotionally drained by the process. Many just give up!' (Munro 1991)

Many professionals feel threatened by family advocacy. Parents can be perceived as loose cannons waiting to go off. They may ask searching questions about the professional's own training, competence and knowledge base. Increasing access to the internet means they can get hold of information of which the professionals are ignorant. It could mean having to accept parents and other relatives as colleagues. Parents can by-pass the usual formal bureau-cratic channels, reach and influence senior managers and elected councillors, often speaking effectively with passion and relevance on behalf of their children. However they are usually, especially and very understandably in the case of children, concerned with 'what is best for the client/child' rather than what that individual wishes, the rightful focus of advocacy.

- Professional advocates: There is a rapidly growing independent professional tradition specialising in areas of disability – the lawyer, the barrister, the ombudsman, guardians ad litem...

39

- What skills do these people have? How can the activities of these increasingly influential professionals be held firmly under the control of people with disabilities? They can easily be tempted into different forms of imperialism.

The rapidly increasing growth of professional advocacy could improve overall efficacy but damage any attempts at maintaining some elements of accountability. To what extent is there an ambulance chasing element? The practice of disability law gives expanding opportunities for money and influence. For example the scandal enquiries are becoming enormously expensive. The Waterhouse Report cost over £13.5 million pounds and the additional monies for the Welsh 'Children First' service amount to only £5 millions. (*The Guardian* 16 February 2000)

Bateman (1995 p. 11) outlines some features of legal representation.

Table 3.1 : Legal Advocacy

• Usually based on a contractual or financial relationship.
• Nature of the problem may involve advocacy that becomes remote from the client.
• Difficult for most to engage in because of complex rules of conduct and limited rights of audience before courts.
• Not concerned with the non-legal aspects of advocacy.
• Highly effective when used to push back the boundaries of the legal understanding of people's rights.

One rapidly expanding example of such advocacy are the Ombudsman posts, pioneered in Scandinavia. Norway was one of the first countries to establish such posts. The first Norwegian Ombudsman wrote movingly:

...the Office has the interests of the child, and no other interest, at heart. This means that we are not suspected of serving other purposes. It also means that we have no obligation to balance the interests of the child against the interests of other groups, such as the elderly. (Flekkoy 1989 p. 116)

However one of her Swedish colleagues writes worryingly: ...our main aim is to improve the society so that every child can grow up in a good environment and be able to develop into a well integrated adult. (Ronstrom 1989 p. 123)

It is hard to take these advocates very seriously. The whole core of advocacy practice is that it doesn't exist separately from the mess of oppressive forces. Being an advocate does mean continually looking over one's shoulder; being under threat from usually powerful forces; experiencing direct vilification from those protecting vested interests like Perceval did. Those responses have an extremely powerful influence on our behaviour and actions as professionals. To think they don't is to be dangerously naïve.

- *Collective advocacy*: this involves a bringing together of people who have similar concerns to change legislation; to press government for more resources; to redress collective wrongs. This uses lobbying to pressurise influential people who might bring about a difference. Methods stretch from passive to extremely active interventions. Often and confusingly, as we have seen already, truly collective advocacy organisations like Survivors Speak Out and People's First are entitled 'self-advocacy' groups.

If devalued individuals are to get any genuine hearing, it is essential that they form groups. Remaining isolated they can rarely be heard. Their power source must increasingly lie in their numbers and activities.

People cannot question the assumptions of the dominant groups in their society all by themselves. To formulate new ways of doing things and set them in motion they need the support of other people who share their perception of the world and help them to challenge the conventional wisdom: "a resistance movement" of some sort. Women have been quite successful in doing this. Black minorities in a white world have found it harder, but not impossible. Many other oppressed groups have yet to gain an effective hearing. (Donnison 1991)

If you cannot get admission to the club that everyone else attends, you must form one of your own. These clubs or groups have their own dangers; they can easily become a source of secondary stigma, hence the essential wisdom of Groucho Marx's refusal to join any club that would have him as a member. There is a delicate balance between the risk of further stigmatisation and the positive gains coming from joint support and action.

Collective advocacy involves quite different skills and different settings from the work with individuals. The relevant tasks and processes are also usually very different. It comes closer to what is more usually described as 'community action.' It involves less emphasis on individual representation and much more on lobbying – pressing politicians and professionals for better and improved conditions, linked with increased resources. It focuses on general issues rather than on the problems of individuals. It means a lot of committee work; taking the chair at meetings; managing finances; writing up minutes; planning press handouts and media impact to influence policies and strategies; learning how to communicate ideas; negotiating and compromising; working in groups creatively; mounting successful campaigns. It is essentially structural and political; doing deals amid the balancing of competing interests.

One example of more collective advocacy are *patients councils*, brought in from The Netherlands in the mid eighties. (Brandon 1991). These provide collective representation for patients in hospitals and sometimes in community based facilities. They attempt to bring about changes in power structures and influence major policy decision making. Their functions cover passive to active roles.

Table 3.2 : Passive - Active roles

• Compiling relevant information.
• Contact with outside bodies.
• Listening to feedback from users.
• Recording what's working well/badly.
• Liaison with complaints/advocacy services.
• Discussions and decisions in the various committees.
• Inform powerful persons about collective grievances.
• Monitor their responses or lack of them.
• React to proposals drafted by powerful people.
• Consult with them.
• Exercise vetoes over defined decisions.
• Active policy making through boards and committees.
• Make specific proposals for change.
• Achieve significant changes through reflecting users' views.

There was a long history of lobbying for macro changes in social work. The influential nineteenth century Barnetts urged 'with ceaseless persistency that what was wanted was not palliatives for personal suffering but remedies for social disease.' They established Toynbee Hall in the East End of London, an important part of the university settlement movement. The basic idea was that residents living in the settlement 'take up some citizen's duty which brings him into contact with others and puts him into a position to learn and to teach.' This was part of an attempt to put middle class leaders in positions of leavening power and influence in lower class areas, to provide leadership and value, and has echoes in the late twentieth century citizen advocacy movement. Pressing politically for better conditions was an important strategy in both their work and what later became established as community work.

Summarise

So we've examined the various types of advocacy and observe some of the patchwork of origins, influences, strengths and weaknesses. Ramcharan has a very useful diagram of these various types and concerns. (Ramcharan 1995 p. 225). Implicit in his diagram is the considerable confusion and tensions we've tried to describe.

Table 3.3 : Advocacy categories

For whom?	Individual, group, self, class (e.g. elderly).
For what?	Services, service inclusion, service quality, Legal rights, life and health, a valued life and image, extension of community connectedness, increases in social security.
Towards or against whom?	Institutions, other agencies, functionaries, families, other individuals.
By whom?	Paid profession,(e.g. lawyer), citizen collectives (e.g. Age Concern), service workers, pressure groups (Grey Panthers), unpaid citizens?
How done?	Persuasion, education, confrontation, litigation, demonstration, modelling, whistle-blowing.

There has been a regrettable trend for advocacy to splinter into a million fragments. It is pulled in so many diverse directions; towards both specialist client groups and also towards the different and sometimes warring methods. So in most towns and cities, we have this delicate and fragile advocacy process battling, largely unsuccessfully, against almost overwhelming odds and concentrated in smaller and smaller pieces like, for example, a partnership advocacy project for elderly people, fighting yet other fragments for increasingly scarce resources.

We can see from this brief look at the various types that they are influenced by a variety of different ideas and have origins at different times and locations. For some – the expressive features – getting to know people, especially those with little recognised communication – warmth and respect is of central importance. Whilst for others, like legal advocacy – 'winning' the particular case, the instrumental features are all important and empowerment may not hold centre stage.

Another differing feature is contextualisation. Some advocates see the individual case as a single example of much more widespread oppressive practice and, like MIND in the 1970s and 1980s looking to see collective redress through the representation of aggrieved individuals. They contextualise the person and develop an accommodation between individual and collective advocacy. Other systems, like partnership advocacy, seem largely unconcerned about any such links and seek the social inclusion of the excluded and devalued individual, through modern versions of casework. Their emphasis goes on re-valuing through social role valorisation, not on accessing rights through active representation.

Chapter 4
SOCIAL WORK AND ADVOCACY

Placing advocacy at the heart of social work has had many doughty opponents. There were historically extremely powerful forces attempting to individualise social issues and these still have their proponents.

> *There can be no doubt that the poverty of the working class is due, not to their circumstances (which are more favourable than those of any other working population of Europe); but to their improvident habits and thriftlessness. If they are ever to be more prosperous, it must be through self-denial, temperance and forethought.* (Charity Organisation Society 1881 p.50)

The poor were to blame for their own poverty and the nature of the interview was interrogation.

Few went quite as far as the 1870s Elberfeld system in Germany, but many had sympathies. 'In the first place the applicant for relief is subjected to an examination so close and searching, so absolutely inquisitorial, that no man who could possibly escape from it would submit to it.'(Brandon 1995). A very long way from advocacy! Social and economic structures were seen as either irrelevant or of very secondary importance. This closely relates to some debates dominating the latter half of the twentieth century – structural versus individual blame and responsibility.

Nineteenth century social caseworkers saw themselves with a more pedagogic function. The nineteenth century social reformer, Octavia Hill wrote, 'Where a man persistently refuses to exert himself, external help is worse than useless'(Brandon and Atherton 1997 p.8) and

> *The people's houses are bad, because they are badly built and arranged, they are tenfold worse because the tenants' habits and lives are what they are. Transplant them tomorrow to healthy and commodious houses, and they would pollute and destroy them.* (Ibid p.9)

This is based almost on a 'contagion' view. The early Charity Organisation Society volunteers, later the paid caseworkers, were bringing a superior morality, a better way of living to those in poverty. They were missionaries rescuing the indigent through example, interviewing and teaching. The first appointment of a health related social worker was Mary Stewart, seconded from the COS, at the Royal Free Hospital in London in 1895, amongst whose functions was to protect the hospital managers from patients 'causing a nuisance'– the converse of advocacy! (Brandon and Atherton 1997).

Other strands of social work had rather more structural perspectives. The profession became immersed in self-doubt, especially after the two World Wars, and wondered increasingly about the impact of socio-economic factors.

> *Some radical social workers are coming to doubt the extent to which a middle-class expert in human relations can help a family living in poverty and bad housing in an urban environment which offers them little escape from the worst that society has to offer... These critics... point out that much of what goes on appears to represent the imposition of the norms of social and family life of the dominant classes upon disadvantaged groups.* (Jordan 1972 p.18)

This was a direct attack on a deeply embedded ideology; almost a social work icon.

Exhortations to advocacy have become prolific in the social work literature. Echoing Elizabeth Fry, the nineteenth century pioneer, the influential Barclay report commented:

> *Social workers would be failing in their duty if they did not speak out in the light of their personal knowledge and the evidence amassed from contact with such (poor and disadvantaged) people, challenging... policy decisions or the way resources are allocated.* (Barclay 1982)

> *When social isolation and professional fragmentation, bureaucracy, dehumanization of clients, or residual orientation deter or prevent those needing help from seeking assistance, skilled social work advocacy may dictate partisanship with the client, with the potential client who hurts but cannot identify a problem or with the delivery of services by non-professionals.* (Haeuser 1976 p.103)

A United Nations document states categorically:

> *Human rights are inseparable from social work theory, values and ethics, and practice. Rights corresponding to human needs have to be upheld and fostered, and embody the justification and motivation for social work action. Advocacy of such rights must therefore be an integral part of social work, even if in countries living under authoritarian regimes such advocacy can have serious consequences for social work professionals.* (United Nations 1994)

As we've seen such advocacy can have very serious consequences even for those working in non-totalitarian regimes.

One early classic American textbook described the development of collective advocacy.

> *Because people need help in simply finding community services within the complex organization of our cities, social workers explored the role of guide, or **broker**, by offering intensive information about services. When this proved inadequate, a more aggressive role of **advocate** was defined. The social worker became a partisan in the conflict and a forceful defender of the client group's point of view. Working now in a political environment, many social workers became increasingly concerned with strategy, negotiation, and the use of conflict.* (Bartlett 1970 p.186)

Whatever the response of these social workers, most social work texts have been vague about the nature of advocacy or representation. Exceptionally, the only social worker to become Prime Minister, Clement Attlee, in his book 'The Social Worker', published in 1920, stated firmly that social workers were advocates (Bateman 1991). A classic text comments

> *...questions of environmental effects on personality and environment as a dynamic in change led to the issue of the caseworker as advocate... (There is) a distinction between 'case advocacy' (caseworker as advocate of societal or agency policy change) ...caseworkers have been and continue to be advocates for their individual clients... it has been an ingredient in treatment throughout the history of case work.* (Roberts and Nee 1970 in Bateman 1995)

In a United States study, almost 90 percent of social workers reported involvement in advocacy as part of their job but less than 1 percent considered themselves full-time advocates (Ezell 1994 pp. 36–46). We sent out questionnaires to all students passing the Diploma in Social Work course at Anglia Polytechnic University. This cohort of 57 people had by then been practising for about twenty months. Asked: 'What proportion of your work involves advocacy?' A few (6) saw advocacy as completely integrated – "In some form or another potentially – all." 17 saw it in the range of 50 per cent – 75 per cent. "I thought a quarter but now realise it's half or more! Interesting!" "Difficult to quantify. Advocate on behalf of clients depending on their ability to communicate, level of family support etc." For 30 it involved less than 50 percent although some responses were complex. "Directly less than 25 per cent but indirectly I view all my work as a type of advocacy." (Brandon and Morris 1996)

Most contemporary social work commentators nowadays perceive advocacy as a core function. Payne comments strongly, 'Social work includes advocacy because it's role is to define needs and individualise clients on the basis of evidence so that, within organisational structures, client's demands can be appropriately represented.'(Payne 1991 p.34) Haynes notes ambivalence in writing about political social work and advocacy especially in training. 'The history of social work's connection to advocacy is juxtaposed onto today's reality of the preponderance of social work education curricula...'(Haynes 1996)

Payne echoes that same ambivalence mentioned in our introduction.

> *Advocacy is a crucial element of all social work for two reasons. First, it is an important and rather neglected skill which although recognised, has not received its place in most general accounts of social work practice. Second and most importantly, it is an essential element in social work's knowledge structure which defines the characteristics of social work.* (Payne 1991 pp. 33–4)

Bateman notes in a similar vein, 'Given that advocacy is part of the social work task, it is depressing that there is so little training or literature available to help social work staff develop effective advocacy skills.'(Bateman 1991).

Some observers have seen it as part of social casework. Simon notes '...questions of environmental effects on personality and environment as a dynamic in change led to the issue of the caseworker as advocate...'He also makes a distinction between 'case advocacy'– pleading for an individual client and 'policy advocacy'– arguing for social and agency changes, that has echoes of the now more commonly used self and collective terms. (Simon quoted in Bateman 1995 p.15). His use of the medical term 'treatment', common in casework theories, was stretched elastically to include the treatment of both systems and structures.

The core of social work advocacy was helping the client to gain more resources and what Davis calls 'poverty work' (Davis and Wainwright 1996). Such work faces strong opposition from those perpetuating the devaluing processes. 'People like this should be grateful for what they get.' 'It's not our job to tackle poverty.' 'If these people were given more they'd only waste it.'(Ibid p.49). It involves the various stages of increasing poverty awareness and developing anti-poverty action as with welfare rights campaigns.

Modern social work consists of three major conflicting strands: **treatment**; the use of **state authority** and **advocacy**. It is a very considerable understatement to talk of the inherent tensions between the various social work roles – as agents of the state, counsellors and advocates. Concretely it is the fundamental tension of doing 'what is best' for the client contrasted with doing 'what he or she asks to be done'– whether we take instructions or give them. As Timms notes 'The concept of the social worker as an expert purveyor and assessor of requisite services is in conflict with the concept of the social worker as advocate.'(Timms in Dalrymple and Hough 1995 p.135). There is a definite tug of war between the social worker as expert and the perception of the client as someone expert in his or her own life.

In a comment on a client named John, who has mental health problems, Butler and Pritchard categorise the types of social work intervention used.

    a) information gathering.

    b) direct counselling with John and his family.

    c) environmental manipulation.

    d) **advocacy**.

    e) the use of behavioural techniques.

    f) attempt to integrate and co-ordinate (Butler and Pritchard 1983 p.90).

It is entirely insufficient to describe this overall approach outlined above as eclectic; it is completely miraculous. How anyone could use these fundamentally conflicting ingredients in working with one individual would be beyond the wit of a committee comprising the Buddha, Christ and Mohammed.

Rose comments forcibly on these conflicting pressures:

> *Social work has been embedded in a structural contradiction since its professional origins. The nature of this contradiction arises from the social historical fact that the profession receives both its legitimation and primary funding from the capitalist state, the same structural base that creates the poverty and abuses of its clients. The profession has been able to avoid or deny its internal contradiction through the adaptation or development of individual defect explanatory paradigms to guide its practice. Whether the guiding model has been taken from psychiatry, psychodynamic theory, ego psychology, behaviourism, or even more recent progressive psychosocial concepts, the result has been the same – systematic exclusion of the social reality of capitalist structures, ideological forms and processes shaping daily life and individual subjective experience. (Rose 1990)*

These fierce words sum up some basic tensions. The methods of intervention of our profession have largely been based on treatment systems. We have largely borrowed from psychodynamic and other psychotherapeutic ideas for much of the past century. With the mountain of fresh social legislation in the latter half of the twentieth century, seeing our profession as one 'solution', social workers are mostly employed by local authorities. They increasingly work in a legal and bureaucratic framework, based on pathological rather than systems models. Their preferred intervention methods see clients as struggling with personal problems that they need help in solving.

In contrast so much of advocacy is profoundly structuralist, in challenging and uncomfortable ways, which Rose will not let us forget. An understanding of the social and economic oceans in which any person swims is vital. Advocates are trying to prevent the state from further oppressing its citizens, to get them a fairer deal that collectively brings about greater liberation. The other strands of social work can be, and often are – crucial ingredients in the oppression – taking away the children, compulsory admission to mental hospital... Treatment can pressurise and manipulate clients to make individual adaptations to the 'real' and overwhelmingly unfair world. This can become a collusion rather than a collision with injustice. The use of authority is assisting the state to screw even more of its citizens, even more effectively.

For Rose, advocacy empowerment strategies contain efforts 'to combat the socially structured alienation, isolation, and poverty of substantive content available to understand ourselves and daily life'. Where clinical models of social work 'inadvertently reproduce the feeling of powerlessness, the experience of oneself as inadequate, incompetent or crazy, even when adaptation to client roles may promote immediate or short-term relief and the appearance of growth.'In great contrast an advocacy/empowerment approach involves 'developing consciousness and active participation in shaping one's life through creating and shaping networks and of social support and action.'(Rose 1990 pp. 41–52)

Rather than developing a genuine concern with the liberation of the oppressed and the personal as political, social work has become embedded in an establishment culture. It has become co-opted. Francis comments:

Legal sanction dominates social work rather than practical and humane "intervention" on behalf of people who have social needs. Such sanctions allow formal methods of control and containment of need to be exercised rather than individually tailored programmes of

50

social support. This crude approach has obvious attractions in a context where more complex and costly strategies of support would entail empowering people to take control of their own lives. (Francis in Northern Curriculum Development Project 1991 p.185)

The covert aim of such systems can be to pacify and persuade to comply with powerful and unfair demands.

Like Francis, Solomon was primarily concerned with racial discrimination. She saw social work as dealing poorly with power blocks. She saw the aims of empowerment as:

Table 4.1 Empowerment aims

• Helping clients to see themselves as *causal* agents in finding solutions to their problems.
• Helping them to see that social workers had a knowledge and skills they could use.
• To see social workers as peers and partners in solving problems.
• To understand the power structure as complex and partly open to influence.

To help achieve these various aims, according to Solomon, the non-racist practitioners require very considerable sensitivity and abilities. They need to join the battle with sword in hand and stand firmly on the right side of the barricades. This means rejecting colonialist explanations of poverty and disability.

- The ability to see alternative explanations for any behaviour, and especially those alternatives we might want to reject as false.

- The ability to use many cues to choose the alternative explanation which is most relevant to the client.

- The ability to feel warmth, genuine concern and empathy regardless of race or other characteristics.

- The ability to confront clients when true feelings of warmth have been misinterpreted or distorted. (Solomon 1976).

In practical terms, social workers are grappling with five dimensions of power – **physical; resource; position; expert; personal**. (Handy 1985) **Physical** power centres on coercion or the perceived threat of it, for example arising from sections of Children's legislation and compulsory admission to psychiatric facilities. **Resource** is the power of the social worker as a gateway (or otherwise) to a variety of services. **Position** involves power arising from the various roles the social worker represents and is closely linked to resources and the right to give or withhold information. **Expert** derives from established specialist experience. **Personal** is concerned with power of personality or charisma. Their various encounters ordinarily reflect a gross imbalance in power relations in all of these areas.

Rees notes some issues about encounters between professionals and clients.

The meetings between social workers and their prospective clients have shown that the provision of "help" depended on the ability of the layman to project and the professional to recognise worthy "moral character". To each social worker these features constitute evidence that such clients merited his commitment of time and the provision of appropriate "resources". By contrast, some people were considered unworthy. Social workers felt little, if any, obligation to help. (Rees 1978 p.107)

This contains some powerful echoes of the nineteenth century casework traditions, examined earlier. Octavia Hill still lives on!

The situation in some areas was even worse. Not only were clients socially invisible and neglected but were actively abused by those designated to help.

...disabled people, and disabled children in particular, have been invisible, both in society and in child protection procedures and practice. This is especially true for black disabled children and those from other minority communities...disabled children are, without doubt, being abused, in many different ways and by many different people. (Westcott and Cross 1996 p.129)

Our overall contention is that the abuse and neglect of devalued individuals is not extraordinary.

As we have seen earlier, there is a very long history of recurring scandals involving sexual and other abuse by workers. The various official enquiries have had a considerable impact on this vulnerable profession. The most recently published is the Waterhouse report. As noted earlier, the original whistle-blower (a social worker) was suspended and eventually sacked from her post. This experience is not at all untypical. A recent survey of social workers showed a great reluctance to bring attention to breaches in care standards. 'Victimisation, mentioned by almost 25 per cent of respondents, is still one of the greatest deterrents to raising concerns.'(Hunt 1998 p.161)

..those who do complain must be courageous, naïve or vengeful. There is absolutely no point in pretending that complaining is easy. Staff must go in to it with their eyes wide open. (Ibid p.163)

There is considerable evidence that colleagues are generally unforgiving of those seen as 'rocking the boat'.

One heartening development is the growth of advocacy groups representing ethnic minorities. Awaaz user's group was set up in 1994.

There had been and still is very low take up of psychiatric services by Asian people living in North Manchester. Professionals were of the opinion that Asian people support each other very well and used this to explain the low uptake of psychiatric services.

Awaaz developed a network partly based on peer advocates. 'Advocates were users or ex-users of mental health services and knew not only the system but had the added advantage of knowing the cultural and linguistic background.'(Awaaz website 1999)

Existing services presented considerable challenges to advocates. In our peer advocacy work with homeless people, we found that 'unattractive' prospective service users faced many hurdles. Stern commented sardonically 'Homeless people fail to consider the needs of the service.'and goes on to say 'services still tend to discriminate against people who make their work more difficult.'This discrimination took many forms but especially: rigid appointments systems in unwelcome settings; fragmented service delivery – for example alcohol, drugs services; provided by geographically dispersed services detached from welfare rights, employment and housing; stigmatisation of homeless people; poor communications between services; idiosyncratic use of care programme approaches.'(Stern 1994 pp. 173–182) We faced similar resistances in getting local mental health services to take people off the streets.

Black asks social workers to recognise these various hurdles and to turn strongly away from the treatment models, where people were seen as having personal difficulties – as problematic – towards advocacy, to become part of the solution rather than the problem.

...typical clinical models of social work inadvertently reproduce the feeling of powerlessness, the experience of oneself as inadequate, incompetent or crazy, even when adaptation to client roles may promote immediate or short term relief and the appearance of growth.'

He was stressing the important role of power rather than illness or immaturity.

He argued for three major elements in professional work with service users: **contextualisation, empowerment and collectivity**.

> *Focusing on* **contextualisation**, *on bringing to consciousness both the unique experience of the individual and the social base for that individual's experience, also means that attention must be primarily given to the structural factors which impose dependency...* **empowerment** *means a process of dialogue through which the client is continuously supported to produce the range of possibility that he/she sees appropriate to his/her needs; that the client is the center for all decisions that affect her/his life...* **collectivity** *means that the focus on the social basis of identity and experience is designed to reduce isolation and the terror of experiencing oneself as uniquely defective and stagnant.* (Rose and Black 1985)

The client was to be perceived in a specific social and economic *context* of a state that was usually hostile and malignant. They were to be supported to understand the relevant and oppressive forces that surrounded them. They were to gain *empowerment* – the means to explore and deliver possibilities appropriate to their needs. Through *collectivity* they could gain a sense of themselves as part of a group of people rather than as a unique and defective individual.

All that involves a continuing dialogue about empowerment. Freire wrote that

> *...dialogue cannot occur between those who want to name the world and those who do not want this naming – between those who deny other men (sic) the right to speak their word and those whose right to speak has been denied them. Those who have been denied their primordial right to speak their word must first reclaim this right and prevent the continuation of this dehumanizing aggression.* (Freire 1982 p.61)

In social work, this has frequently meant an attempt at dialogue between those chronically unused to talking and expressing their wishes, faced by those professionals and politicians well used to having things their own way.

All this raises huge issues for actual practice. It is extremely difficult to perceive how social workers, in developing this sort of radical practice could avoid regular and even terminal confrontations with their employing authority and the relevant systems. They run the risk of disciplining, unpopularity, exclusion and even dismissal. The very nature of their professional activity, partly operating as agents of the state, poses dangerous paradoxes. Gathercole outlines five different sorts of conflict that lie in wait for even the most wary service professional.

Table 4.2   Advocacy conflicts

Organisational: service survival interests are often seen as more important than user interests. Scandal must be avoided, even at the cost of continuing neglect, abuse or exploitation.

Professional: staff may discourage promotion of users' interests which may challenge the good name of the profession.

Managerial: interests of managers may differ from what grass roots staff see as the interests of users, for example, bonuses paid to health service managers for resettling people from hospitals.

Personal: even if serving only one person, one's own personal needs, for example for rest, may be a source of conflict.

Competition: service workers have competing demands on their time from other residents. (Gathercole 1988 p.13)

Wolfensberger details some of these obstacles and the accompanying self-deceptions:

> *... many benevolent, humanistic clinicians see themselves as servants of the public, offering themselves and their services in a non-controlling fashion. They see their clients as free agents, free to reject the offered services. Their self-concept – in part due to the indoctrination received during training – is frequently compatible with action perceived as controlling, directing or dictating client behaviour. Yet here it is where so many human service workers deceive themselves, because their roles are not only almost always societally sanctioned, but in an endless array of encounters between server and the served, the server is the interpreter of, and agent for the intents of society, and wields a truly amazing amount of power and control, even if he (sic) may not consciously perceive himself as so doing... Indeed, it is not too much to say that who will be rich or poor, health or sick, bright or dumb, honest or crooked – and even born or unborn – depends in many cases, and to a significant extent, upon the decision of human managers.* (Wolfensberger 1972)

Although he is characteristically going over the top, he is describing ideas about largely unconscious and destructive processes that help shape services. Professionals desperately want to believe that they are primarily serving the needs of the clients, when, as realists like Wolfensberger and Gathercole suggest, the structures distort and pollute this genuine compassion. All of us live in a turbulent universe with immense pressures to behave in ways that are far away from the needs of vulnerable people.

Our former Anglia students, now practising as social workers recorded some great tensions. Overall we had 51 comments about conflicts. One person was very sanguine. 'The ideal is never available. Compromise or inability to deliver services is common.' Three saw no conflict 'the old peoples home is an ideal forum for advocacy' and rather more mysteriously, 'No conflicts but plenty of frustrations from within one's own agency – social services.'Nearly half (28) targeted funding as presenting particular problems. 'There is a funding crisis, clients have to stay in hospital until services are ready.' 'Because of the funding problems, the current whip crackers are tending to give agency needs the priority.' 'Resource shortfalls; services are not needs led.' 'Management are purely budget driven.' One complained about the wasteful use of scarce resources: 'Frustration at not being able to provide cost effective services because of the social services policy of using in-house providers.'

Some saw that advocating effectively might adversely affect others. 'Few resources; obtaining more resources for one client means none for another.' 'Limited finances mean you have to rob Peter to pay Paul.' 'Social workers are actively competing against one another for resources.' More generally, there was a difficult balance to be struck. Ten mentioned difficulties with the agency and colleagues. 'You have to present the clients needs but are also expected to maintain the departments policies.' More concretely, 'I found it hard to reconcile a policy of home closure with the needs of the elderly residents.' 'Career prospects could be blighted if you became too vociferous and deemed "difficult" to work with.' 'There is very little support for the advocacy role in the social services department.' But five others felt supported. 'My agency actively encourages advocacy.' Ten had conflicts with parents and carers. 'Relatives demand: 'Let's put them in a home' when they only need meals on wheels.' 'No mechanism for parents to define their needs; conflicts between parents and their children's needs.' 'Are we advocates for the child or parents – often conflicts, problems with court proceedings?' (Brandon and Morris 1996)

Muriel Ball was a social worker and writes passionately about her frustrations.

> *My feeling is that you cannot practise true advocacy when you have to work within an organisation that has policies. In the final analysis you are expected to follow the party line. As a social worker I had to adapt myself to my organisation or else get out, which is what I eventually chose to do. I think that* **professionals cannot do true advocacy and represent the individual in ways that make total change.** *The professionals have to*

leave on one side very great areas of conflict and are constantly at risk of being seen as no longer members of the team. (quoted in Teasdale 1998 p.107)

She is referring vaguely to 'true', sometimes called 'pure' advocacy, client representation that has no or few conflicts and tensions. Whilst extremely sympathetic to the everyday frustrations she describes, we have considerable doubts as to whether 'true' advocacy did or indeed can ever exist.

There are some who take the view that advocacy is not a 'true' social work activity. The problem with this belief is that it does not reflect the needs of social work consumers, nor does it acknowledge the fact that much social casework is, inevitably, tied up with advocacy. For example, a decision concerning a child's placement with foster parents will mean advocating which type of placement is best for them. (Bateman 1991)

This accurately reflects the expressed wishes of many consumers that social workers will be a voice for them but confuses 'what is best for them' with taking instructions. This is all the more disturbing because Bateman is the prime proponent of what he calls 'principled advocacy'– 'the principles used are based on some of the professional conduct rules of solicitors.'

Bateman identifies some ground rules for advocacy, as follows.

Table 4.3   Advocacy ground rules

* Act in the service user's best interests.
* Keep the service user properly informed.
* Act only in accordance with his/her instructions.
* Carry out those instructions with diligence and competence.
* Give no advice on matters in which they are not competent (Bateman 1991).

It is unclear what happens if service users give instructions that are not in their best interests and, after discussion, insist on those instructions. Who decides what is in the 'best interests' of the client? If the social worker/advocate thinks that the client is in self-destruct mode, do they refuse to act on behalf of him or her; insist on making a case that is, in their view, helpful?

In a later work, Bateman is clearer and even more disturbing.

> *Acting in the client's interests may also mean that the advocate has to steer away the client away from a particular course of action that the client would like to pursue – for example, where the suggested course of action is likely to have a detrimental physical, material or psychological effect, or where the same result could be achieved through another course of action... What if the clients best interests are not in the best interests of society or a wider group of clients?* (Bateman 1995 pp. 27–8)

We have suggested throughout this book that the advocate has no business playing about in areas of assumed divinity. Bateman takes us right back to aspects of social casework – what we've called the helicopter position. It is very hard to agree with him that 'the client is now in the driving seat rather than being driven along by the professional desires of the helper.' (Bateman 1995, p.29) It is certainly the role of the advocate to raise issues of concern about proposed strategies and to engage in a discussion about the consequences of such actions and to explore possible alternatives. After all this exploration and discussion, the advocate must decide whether to put up or shut up; whether he can represent the client on his terms, to take his or her instructions.

Arnstein makes an extremely helpful distinction between four different levels of involvement in decision making, teasing out some of the issues raised by Bateman and O'Sullivan.

Table 4.4 Level of client involvement

<table>
<tr><td>

Being told
The client(s) is not involved in the decision making process but is informed that their child is being taken in to care; they are to be admitted compulsorily to mental hospital – and may also have explained as to why. They are the passive recipients of information.

Being consulted
The client(s) is asked their opinion and this gets fed into the decision making process that may be taken into account but not necessarily acted on. The actual decision is made in a setting and place, even involving unseen others, not accessible to them.

Being a partner
Decisions are jointly made between the client(s) and the professionals subject to an agreement. However this sort of partnership often involves a considerable power imbalance and even relevant documents that may be unavailable to the client concerned.

</td></tr>
</table>

Being in control
The client makes the decisions, with or without the facilitation of the social worker. They clearly have the control, as with direct payments systems. (Arnstein 1969 pp. 216–24)

Professionals face all sorts of institutional hurdles to the involvement of service users. The rules and regulations of their agencies make it often almost impossible for social workers to involve them fully in decisions that might result, for example, in court action; the use of statutory powers; the confidentiality of a third party... Our Anglia research showed that advocacy was just a single ingredient in a very complicated intervention process, that usually engages with other professionals who do not share those approaches. Although these social workers had an advocacy role, they were not advocates. Their other roles, arising from treatment and state agency responsibilities, forced a move between the four elements outlined above.

Aside from these systemic obstacles there are many others that can inhibit power transfers. O'Sullivan makes a list including: 'being a danger to self and others; age and understanding of children; incapacity to make decisions; fairly and unfairly distributing resources; some clients may not want to be involved.' (O'Sullivan 1999 pp. 50–53). More generally where power is centralised, as in many day and residential services, the face-to-face staff may have very little real power themselves as major decisions are made at the head offices. If you don't have the power, you can't give it away!

It is our contention that advocates can operate only within the last of the four stages. They are working within a framework that gives the client the control. They have no business working in the other zones. We have already seen how difficult this posture is, within the existing professionalised hegemonies.

Some observers see this primary concern, even sometimes described as an obsession, with rights – as misguided. Marsland argues that there should be a decisive shift away from rights, towards the education of social workers in skills that help their clients become increasingly self-reliant and less dependent on the state (Marsland in Denney 1998). This position stresses responsibilities as opposed to rights and is deeply concerned with the growth of the dependency culture – the so-called Nanny State. Relying on paid others is perceived as highly undesirable. Dependency and rights are placed side by side, as if the one encourages the other. We've never seen a greater access to rights as any barrier to the acceptance of social and economic responsibilities.

In some contexts, the professionalised conflicts may be minimal. Some posts contain either as a specific duty to advocate or are even independent or quasi-independent – as in the Guardians Ad Litem positions. Guardians Ad Litem working with children have a very high degree of independence. Their role was considerably changed towards helping to empower some children perceived as being at risk.

> *The basic responsibility of the guardian is to safeguard the child's interest in any proceedings brought. To this end the guardian is directed to give first and paramount consideration to the needs of the child, at the same time taking in to account their wishes and their feelings and having regard to the child's age and understanding... This approach then requires the guardian to become a mediator, negotiator, resource broker, case manager and monitor.* (Kerr and Gregory 1998 p.1)

Terms like 'mediator' and phrases like 'taking in to account' communicate vestiges of the helicopter function – 'acting in the best interests' that are difficult to reconcile with basic advocacy principles.

The Police and Criminal Evidence Act 1984 involves social workers and nurses in advocacy roles, under the 'appropriate adult' clause, in safeguarding vulnerable persons, whilst held in police custody.

> *In the case of persons who are mentally ill or mentally handicapped it may, in certain circumstances be more satisfactory if the 'appropriate adult' is someone who has experience of training in their care rather than a relative lacking in such qualifications.* (Brandon 1995 p.37)

We have much sympathy with the comments of Alison Taylor, a social worker. 'Modern social work appears to bend to whatever social, penal and economic ideologies are dominant. Its purpose is unclear, it has no independent goals or standards, and its responses are reactive and crisis driven.' (Taylor in Hunt 1998 p.45). Two years ago we protested vigorously against the introduction of a compliance policy drafted by a local authority social services department. The aim of this policy seemed to be to compel conformity and crush potential whistle-blowers. The draft policy was eventually withdrawn.

Linked with these naked pressures from a managerialist culture, Hadley and Clough (1996 p.43) describe the model team leader. She

> *doesn't make waves and doesn't criticise the system and doesn't raise her head above the parapet. Someone, I suppose, who goes along with the drift of things. If they bring out a policy that is just unworkable, never say its unworkable. Just accept it and work with it as you can.'*

Powell outlines the conflict between an increasingly managerialist culture in relation to changes in social work.

Central to these changes is the increasing power of managerial ideology, or managerialism. In a managerialist view, management is seen as superior to other forms of organization such as professionalism. The imposition on social work of standardized procedures is one factor which leads to whistleblowing, as bad professional practice can continue so long as it remains within the procedures. The client of traditional social work has become the service user or consumer, reflecting significant changes to the relationship between social worker and client. This professional relationship has been reformed to be represented in the changing environment of social care as being similar to, or even the same as, the relationship of the customer or consumer in a commercial market relationship. (Powell in Hunt 1998 pp. 165–6)

Such a view, as Powell rightly argues, is arrant nonsense. The social work client is in an entirely different situation from the supermarket customer. He or she is not at all sure of the nature of the product, most often shrouded in social service mystery and kept under the counter. He or she has no money to purchase unless they are lucky enough to be amongst the few thousands using a direct payments scheme. He or she is 'shopping' in the only supermarket available to them – a monopolistic social services departmental office. The relationship between these 'customers' and the 'shop assistants' reflects a very considerable imbalance of power. Clients are very strange shoppers!

Professionals opposed to such process are forced into whistleblowing. The United States Federal Whistleblower's Act 1989 defines it as 'the disclosure of information by an employee or ex-employee which they reasonably believe evidences a violation of any law, rule or regulation, or gross mismanagement or gross waste of funds, an abuse of authority or a substantial and specific danger to public health and safety.' Reactions to this sort of advocacy have been overwhelmingly hostile, as we know from personal experience. It has been seen as destructive and injurious.

Atkinson is quite clear. 'Social workers are not advocates (although they may have an advocacy role)...'She suggests that advocates may fill the gaps left by the statutory services 'as they concentrate on community care assessments and bought in packages of care'. She even suggests somewhat extravagantly that advocates 'offering a wide range of practical and emotional support to the disadvantaged vulnerable people may be re-inventing social work.'(Atkinson 1999 p.34)

A series of important questions lie buried here, some investigated earlier. The first looks at the dangers of advocacy stretching itself across a wide range of roles – including the primarily expressive and whether any individual professional can be effective in all these very different areas. The second is whether there is a valid distinction to be made between being an advocate and having an 'advocacy role.' This revolves again around the elusive concept of 'pure' or 'true' advocacy. How do social workers see the situation?

Beresford provides a wiser view than Atkinson.

> *Can professionals be advocates? Yes, but when they have power over individual service users, or responsibilities other than to speak for the person, then there is a conflict of interest, and the person will need an independent advocate. But at all times service workers need to have some awareness of, and try to protect the service user's interests (however imperfectly they do this, given conflicts of interest) and not just leave this to the advocate.* (Beresford 1994)

This is an eminently sensible view of existing realities.

Our former students are wise. They made a valuable distinction between internal and external work. Forty-nine specified particular issues about insider advocacy. At the two extremes were – 'not sure whether this is truly possible within my employing agency – my role as an employee would prevent being able to take on the advocacy' and 'arguing with and challenging management decisions about care packages; pushing for increased services.' Twenty-one mentioned resources and money specifically. 'making a case for money; memos to budget holders, involves good assertiveness and communication skills, knowledge about eligibility criteria.' Eighteen mentioned expressing client's views to managers and colleagues. 'Challenging colleagues about oppressive practice.' Twelve saw case conferences, reviews and team meetings as major places for representation. 'Advocacy through case discussions with colleagues and managers.' 'Advocating for clients at team meetings.' Two mentioned helping users to make complaints about the services and colleagues.

Forty-seven gave specific answers about advocating externally, dominated by social security and housing issues. They intervened because 'other agencies respond more positively to us than to clients.' 'I'm helping people obtain their rights and needs.' They were most usually 'informing clients of their rights, providing written reports and making phone calls to press their case with other agencies.' Twenty-one mentioned housing authorities, perceived as external agencies. They struggled to 'ensure that families receive all their rights and obtain appropriate housing.' 'Ringing housing departments to get more points.'

Eighteen specifically mentioned social security. One person had represented a client at a social security tribunal. 'It is difficult with social security as they won't discuss individual cases.' Health Service colleagues rarely got mentioned – twice for nurses, one each for physiotherapists and G.P.s. Charities and solicitors were noted once. Education came up three times: 'Met teachers to support child getting back into school.' Several (7) supported self advocates. 'Encouraging users to self advocate.' 'Offer support to clients to represent themselves for example in the problems of access to medical records.'

Few social work texts can be described as seminal but certainly Mayer and Timms''The Client Speaks' can. (Mayer and Timms 1970). It is a detailed study of 61 former users of a Family Welfare Association (FWA – the direct successor to the Charity Organisation Society) service. Many users were critical of the 'treatment' offered. Re-reading this fascinating research, we are surprised that it never occurred to the authors that these service users were receiving treatment when they were asking for representation. They were expecting the caseworker to do something. They received a form of treatment, influenced by psychodynamic theories but many may have wanted some form of advocacy.

Until more is known about the nature and source of the problem-solving views held by working-class people, nothing definite can be said about the likelihood of successfully 'resocialising' them. (Mayer and Timms 1970, p.145)

'Resocialising' has powerful echoes of Octavia Hill and is a long way off from Freire, Rose and Black – and other exponents of empowerment. Some clients receiving weekly insight therapy from the FWA were asking for material support and helpful representation in accessing housing resources. They were asking for advocacy. 'My sister said: "My God, you don't expect that they are going to give you money at the FWA, do you! They are just there to talk to."' (Ibid p.134). The approaches then preferred by the FWA indicated profound and dangerous disrespect of the client's own definitions of their personal problems. These involved an overall assumption that the more profound and relevant reasons for their difficult situations and relationships lay outside the direct knowledge of the distressed individual and within the competence of the professional. This resonates with comments made by Bateman quoted earlier in this section, implying responsibilities of the advocate for issues, invisible to the client. These processes threaten to take us faraway from taking instructions and genuinely empowering vulnerable others.

Robinson comments relevantly and sardonically.

> *The social worker should have the long-term goal of changing this social system and his actions should be strategically directed to this end. There is consequently a major emphasis on the need to raise the client's 'level of consciousness' so that he sees the wider causes of his problems and begins to fight to change them rather than just improve his personal lot. Ironically, advocates of this approach share in common with psychodynamically oriented social workers a conviction that they know better than the client and must therefore help him to achieve 'insight'. They simply differ about the content of the insight.*
> (Robinson 1978, p.29)

Social Work's involvement in advocacy is very complex. It contains many dimensions and mixtures around whether the advocacy is about macro or micro issues and also whether direct or indirect.

Table 4.5   Social work advocacy involvement

Representing clients directly
Micro: advocate for a client trying to access social security benefits; writing to a housing office making a case for housing transfer.

Macro: whistleblowing about deficiencies in whole services (for example, the Waterhouse inquiry); lobbying or collectively advocating for improved welfare rights, better facilities for immigrants; changes in social legislation.

Supporting advocacy indirectly
Micro: supporting self-advocacy, backing up a client complaining about services; working with a self-advocacy group; advocacy component in care planning – basing the plan more on what the client wants than on some notion of 'needs'.

Macro: helping neighbourhood groups to articulate deficiencies in the collection of rubbish and repair to damage done by vandals.

Many of our former Anglia students had considerable contact with other advocates. This included lawyers, CAB, Ombudsman and family members. 'I use CAB most days to check on the law.' 'CAB is very helpful.' 'Many young people have lawyers to defend them in court against criminal charges.' Lawyers were most criticised (7). 'They operate in a narrow legalistic framework often not in the *best interests* of clients.'

Families were a common form of advocacy. 'Families are often very concerned about the bullying of their children, advocate for their children at the school or in the neighbourhood.' 'Relatives are the main advocates for those with learning difficulties.' Their major activity was to 'express the needs of the relative' and 'complain about service deficiencies.' Some respondents (11) noted tensions. 'Parents advocate for the child but sometimes this conflicts with what he or she wants.' 'Family advocates are highly relevant in the mental health field although may not always *have the best interests* of the clients.' 'Families see themselves as advocates sometimes but often to get what they want rather than to meet the needs of the client.'

Chapter 5
ADVOCACY STAGES

The measurement of the various kinds of advocacy is not easy but reasonably simple. It is very curious that such measurements are studiously avoided by both researchers and advocacy agencies. For example, the recent NHS mental health national service framework states that advocacy arrangements should be provided but nowhere describes what they should do or how they should or could be measured. (Department of Health 1999 p. 10)

We have preciously few systematic evaluations of the effectiveness of the advocacy process, partly – as we've seen – because it is so ill-defined. Another reason might be that at this vulnerable stage in our history, we're afraid to face up to, what might be, harsh truths. Instead what we have is, all too often, just a series of interesting stories. The acid test is – *does advocacy – either directly by the aggrieved individual or an advocate assisting him or her to get what they want and can it, in its collective form, have an impact on oppressive systems?* This question would examine the tensions between the fundamental expressive and instrumental functions that Wolfensberger delineated.

Of course it is important that people advocating on behalf of themselves or changes in systems or being advocated for, feel respected and valued as with any service. Many vulnerable people lack the confidence or even the abilities to seek support of this kind. Sometimes silence can be evidence of the most profound oppression rather than satisfaction. However the core of the process is that the designated and agreed tasks requested by the service users are accomplished and that makes a valuable distinction from counselling.

The primary 'task' of counselling and psychotherapy is *expressive*, although it may contain some advocacy features. Counselling itself becomes like a piece of elastic, being latterly used by the High Street Banks in the term – financial counselling. However, professionals who are relatively fresh and enthusiastic may attract all sorts of peripheral processes and tasks. They have a polyfilla quality – being used to fill all sorts of holes and gaps. People seeking advocacy are mostly disappointed with the services and may want all sorts of help, ordinarily provided by a wide range of professionals. It is tempting, as we well know, to slip the big S T-shirt on and go to battle!

To considerably sharpen measures of the *instrumental* effectiveness of advocacy, we must be much clearer about the various stages of the process and the different principles expressed. There is a need to keep potentially destructive processes like 'rescuing' in check. Neither the Knights of the Round Table or Superman have a place in advocacy. What are the reasonable expectations and outcomes? These outcomes may differ greatly as to their degree of difficulty. For example, it may be simple to get someone's social security benefits increased but considerably harder to get a housing transfer to a 'better' neighbourhood. It may turn out that the client is entitled to some benefits not yet claimed but the housing transfer depends on many factors outside the control of the advocate.

A casual reader of the blossoming literature might be forgiven for the impression that they've stumbled across the mystical rites of a secret society, even occasionally a coven. Relevant books and magazines regale the thirsty enquirer with long and fascinating stories, often inspirational, but still extremely vague. It is usually difficult to make out what is actually happening and by what means. All or much remains hidden. Nowhere is the flaming sword of confidentiality used more adeptly to conceal ten thousand failures! Ironically this is a group of largely professional people, quite unused to examination and criticism.

Table 5.1   Stages of advocacy

- explain the advocacy process.
- listen to the client's situation.
- explain the relevant systems – complaints procedures, appeals machinery, outline relevant legislation...
- take instructions.
- seek additional information.
- feed back to the client; exploring together the perceived consequences of possible decisions.
- take revised instructions.
- with permission negotiate with influential persons.
- further feedback to client and together explore the consequences.
- prepare for any possible litigation; Ombudsman...
- evaluate the whole process to learn necessary lessons.

These various stages are not obligatory or even necessary and most advocacy will pass through only some. For example, it is probable that advocacy will rarely result in taking legal action or seeking support from the various Ombudsman. An important role of the advocate is to seek accurate information and to constantly feed back in lucid language the constantly changing situation to the client and help them to explore various consequences and the costs of possible actions. This is a complex task often requiring considerable skill, working with vulnerable people who previously have had bad experiences with a variety of professionals. 'Why should you be any different from the others?' is a reasonable question to be asked of an advocate by any client. We saw the work of Adam earlier on 'self-hatred' as an aspect of clientism.

To genuinely empower clients, the whole advocacy process must be carefully *explained* and an atmosphere created based on warmth, respect and trust. This is the foundation for the whole work and involves a genuine partnership, resulting in a transforming dialogue. The client must be given the opportunity to fully understand, largely to address the inherent imbalance of power between him or her and the professional advocate. For some clients that can be a disturbing experience. They are unused to being listened to; to discussing what they really really want. He or she should understand that they are in charge of the process. For some clients this may be very difficult to comprehend. They have become institutionalised, got used to being told what to do, find it hard to know what *they* want, rather than what professionals demand. They have become inculcated into a culture of helplessness. The advocate must strongly resist taking over, getting into authoritarian mode and adding to the disempowerment process.

The advocate must *listen carefully* and treat seriously the description by the client of the situation they face. At all costs they must avoid therapising. In the mental health services there is a great tendency for professionals to get sucked into rows over diagnostic categories or to get seduced into some sort of counselling.

There are three main courses open for the client:

- pursuing self-advocacy, doing it themselves;
- having the advocate in support either with advice off stage or physically being present at meetings but taking a minor role;
- the professional representing them.

As Black demanded earlier, individual struggles become contextualised in the whole advocacy process. In listening to an individual's unique grievances, the advocate relates them to an overall picture of the collective struggle and the whole life of the person. Peter Relton, a user advocate in Bradford sits in on case review meetings in a mental health service based on social disability principles. He comments 'Bizarre behaviour can always be made meaningful if attention is paid to what is going on in an individual's life.' (James 2000)

It may be difficult to communicate with certain individuals and it is the responsibility of the advocate to try with any necessary assistance. This can involve using an interpreter because the client has a hearing impairment or speaks another language. More generally certain sorts of clients are seen as with few communication skills – those with dementia, persistent vegetative states... One of the most disabling barriers faced by people with dementia is the all too common assumption that it is impossible to communicate effectively with them. This often arises in the context of the hopelessness associated with the medical diagnosis.' (Morris 1997 p. 21)

It may well be that someone is unable to communicate in mainstream ways, cannot fully understand what advocacy would involve and that will present difficulties for the whole process but there is usually much more communication than at first realised. Our work with Judith taught us that almost everyone can spit out Kelloggs cornflakes (and in our opinion should). She was young woman with multiple impairments but in working together with her, we could begin to understand slowly both her expressions of joy and sorrow (Brandon 1994). Time brought a deeper appreciation of her life.

The advocate should carefully *explain the relevant machinery* – complaints procedures, pathways for appeals – available to the client and provide the relevant written materials. The documentation is substantial: local authority guidelines and policies; government departmental directives; relevant legal rulings; social security handbooks... Ann McDonald's small book (1997) is especially helpful in areas like care planning and struggling with local authorities. These explanations aim at widening the perceived options and contributing further avenues for possible redress. It is an obligation for an advocate to communicate some of the likely financial and emotional costs of taking up advocacy on a grievance without discouraging them from doing so. Some people we've supported over the years have paid a very considerable cost in time and emotional turmoil.

The advocate should **take instructions**. This sounds reasonably simple but it isn't. He or she is being 'instructed' by the client to undertake certain agreed actions. That means that there has been an exploration and explanation by the advocate and professional in which the client is perceived as the 'dominant' partner. It is their grievance and their life. The advocate acts as a turf accountant never as a tipster, with a task to mark the card of the client with his or her view about whether the runners have long or short odds. What their form is? It is no part of their task to instruct the client which horse to put their money on. There are unusual circumstances where the advocate cannot for reasons of conscience or otherwise go with the client's wishes – then they must decline to act and recommend another advocate.

That process sounds easy but it isn't at all. It is tempting to rush off in a cloud of professionalised jargon and overwhelm the person seeking redress and compound the already existing difficulties and power imbalances. Advocacy is either a process of empowerment or nothing at all. It is about the restless search for liberation and helping people to develop a critical and creative citizenship (Ledwith 1997 p. 139). In the same moment as writing that, yet another yawning chasm appears. It is tempting, often deeply unconsciously, to use clients as pawns in some covert political game – tempting and completely unacceptable for our own ends. Macro versus micro. It is more than tempting, extremely hard to avoid. That is no pursuit of liberty but manipulation falls into the same trap as the therapists. Professionals who claim to know how their clients should live are dangerous.

> *The use of clients by caseworkers in policy advocacy could develop into conscious as well as unconscious exploitation of clients' misery and the helplessness as surely as the goal of adjustment to his environment (which was never a theoretical goal of casework) is alleged to have done. This exploitation will develop unless there is careful work with clients as to what they want for themselves and how much they want to and can involve themselves as citizens, not clients in societal and policy change.* (Simon 1970)

The advocate should make a careful written note of what the client requires to be done, of the relevant instructions and check its accuracy at the end of the session. This may involve actions to be taken directly by the aggrieved individual (self-advocacy) or indirectly (on behalf of the client – professional representation). In studying these notes the advocate should seek for evidence of his or her hidden agendas, of seeking for power, playing some sort of a chess game not relevant to the client's expressed wishes. Our individual preferences as advocates should play very little part in the whole process and this is where regular supervision is vital. If we are unable to accept the client's instructions we should suggest someone else.

These instructions will usually involve seeking out *further information*. There is a vast amount of material buried in a thousand places. The client usually needs additional material, perhaps in terms of legislation or local authority regulations that should be sought. Our experience is that local authorities and health trusts are poor at providing relevant material. Requests are dealt with slowly and reluctantly. The advocate meets a labyrinth that uses the principle of confidentiality as manufactured fog. We had an example last year where a client was refused access to her own care plan on the grounds that it was confidential!

> *Age Concern and Mencap have each produced research which shows that local authorities, despite government guidance to the contrary, are very poor at telling people what they do. The right to information is in this context the basic right on which all others are predicated, and should therefore be the next focus for those who wish to challenge local authority decisions.* (McDonald 1997 p. 73)

Such information is often incomprehensible. It is written in a local authority or health service Greek or Latin, with obscure mnemonics only decipherable by long-term insiders or those fluent in that particular esoteric language. It needs careful translation into easily digestible and understandable forms. Giving people information is rarely the same as informing them.

After this information is discovered or uncovered, it should be *fed back* lucidly to the client and relevant consequences spelled out. This is a vital part of the whole empowerment and liberation process, otherwise we can get in to considerable power imbalances. With the lawyers the clients can easily lose the plot and get taken over, so they don't fully understand what is going on.

Those initial *instructions may then need revision* and this can become a regular loop system. More information leads to changes in posture onward to more information... The client sees fresh possibilities for new and more ambitious pathways and/or serious hurdles obstructing his initial desires.

Negotiation may prove necessary, where relevant and powerful persons are involved in discussions to reach the ends desired by the client. These are shark- infested waters. Negotiation can easily come to tacit agreements between Mafia members (advocates are often tempted into temporary membership!) that are not in the real interests of the client but convenient for everyone else. Advocates can get sucked in to temporary and honorary club membership. 'You seem to be a reasonable person...' One great difficulty in any negotiation is that other professionals have a sketchy understanding of what advocacy is about. One professional commented recently of an advocate: 'She seems to take the part of the client rather than an objective professional stance.' (!)

Dissatisfaction with decisions, especially about social work assessment, can be used to challenge both the social workers and their employing authorities. (McDonald 1997). If the client is not present (because he or she doesn't want to be) the *results of the negotiation are fed back* clearly and fully and may then result in some *fresh instructions* because offers have been made or withdrawn, changing the existing situation. The likely consequences of fresh instructions should be explored.

If negotiation with powerful others is either wholly or partly unsuccessful in the client's view, further negotiation could take place or it might be time to consider a referral to a variety of *Ombudsman* or to consider, if relevant, *litigation*. If and when the client feels it is time to seek other support, there are various local agencies including the Citizen Advice Bureaux that could offer some advice.

Whatever the individual case results, each advocacy experience should be *evaluated*, basically in terms of considering whether or not the stated ends of the client were achieved. All of us are human and have different strengths and weaknesses. We may be better at seeking information than negotiating; more effective over the phone than face to face.

Evaluation involves:

- the need for carefully considered reflection by the advocate with the help of their relevant supervisor, with the integral difficulty in local authority social services departments (and elsewhere) that this person, usually a manager, has very considerable conflicts of interests, especially where the case has involved seeking redress against his or her employing authority, and there is a direct conflict between the rights of the client and the needs as seen by the agency. The Manager may be directly responsible for the oppression experienced by the client.

- the feedback from the client as to how it went, expressively but also and crucially – instrumentally. Did they get what they were hoping in terms of outcomes? Was it possible with better advocacy to get some of the things they hadn't got? What might have been improved and how?

- this particular segment of the evaluative process to be included in the regular annual and external reviews by an independent body into the quality and focus of the work.

Chapter 6
CONCLUSION

Advocacy is very diverse and bewildering. It has a long history but in the last twenty years has splintered into many more methods and systems. It is in greater danger of getting lost and becoming part of the established systems. 'Success' is extremely seductive.

As we've already seen from research at Anglia Polytechnic University, the practise of advocacy or more exactly having an advocacy role, by social workers is healthy and even vigorous. The great majority of these freshly trained professionals see it as an important part of their work. Their interest is not yet reflected in the social work literature, that is to say the least ambivalent about the representation of clients.

This is a profession, like so many others, that is embedded in an entangled web of paradoxes. It contains three major ingredients: treatment; state agent and advocacy. These ingredients are ordinarily in conflict. We manage scarce resources that prevent most clients from getting what they need. We represent 'vulnerable' people who are vigorously socially and economically excluded by the state services that pay most of us. We 'treat' people through counselling interventions, though we know that most of their internal despair is linked with the immense stigma and hurdles coming from the major social structures.

Professionally, we struggle with the notion of 'knowing what is best' for people in poverty as our founding fathers and mothers did. There are some clever new psychological versions of the nineteenth century 'deserving and non-deserving' paradigm. Advocacy can have no truck with this. We don't know how others ought to live; what ways of behaving are mature and immature; what are personality disorders and what are not. It is no part of the role of being an advocate to 'know what is best' for clients. We don't even know what is best for us.

In the broth of social work practice with all its herbs and different flavours, things are very complex. Our particular paradoxical recipes force us to work with disparate and often clashing ingredients. Any social work intervention, as we've seen, is likely to have a heady mixture of counselling, bits of legislation, topped up with homespun advice – offers to mediate and advocate. That can make an almost undrinkable brew. It is a powerful mixture of 'what is best for you'; 'informing about what the state requires, especially what the legislation demands;' and 'standing up for the wishes of the service user'. The potential for conflict is massive.

Advocacy demands that we take seriously the term 'social' in our job title. We need an increased understanding of the person in social and economic context; a determination to work with others to do something about deprivation and distress.

> *Advocacy demands...an understanding of the way in which the client's particular situation is connected to the broader problem of power differentials based on social class, race, gender, age and ethnicity. And advocacy requires courage. It is not easy to be disliked, especially when one is fighting the good fight.* (Wood and Middleton 1991 pp. 53–63)

It is hard to be optimistic about the role of advocacy in social work. Organisations – whether private, voluntary or statutory – find increasingly effective ways of defending themselves against both insiders and outsiders, who are perceived as enemies. They use gagging clauses in employment contracts; improve in handling public relations; develop managerialist cultures based on loyalty to the organisation rather than duties to clients and relatives. The whistleblower is faced with an outer face that professes to value his or her activities but an inner face that is increasingly hostile and considerably cleverer at dealing with dissidents.

Whether optimistic about social work or not, the future for advocacy is immense. It has become a favourite solution in the new joined up services. It has a special if somewhat vague place in the heart of the government's mental health policies. In mental health the Government has showed in the Green Paper on the reform of the Mental Health Act, a strong commitment to clarify the role of advocacy in supporting individuals with mental health needs. There is a push towards independent advocacy systems for all patients subject to the proposed Mental Health Act. The NHS Plan states that by 2002 a nationwide Patient Advice and Liaison Service (PALS) will be established in every NHS Trust beginning with all major hospitals. PALS are not advocates but problem solvers providing a route through provide to independent advocacy. They may have an advocacy role in aiding patients with hospital complaint procedures. In learning difficulties, recent policies focus on the development of 'self' and 'citizen advocacy' and not on models of paid advocacy. The government is committed in the 'Valuing People: A New Strategy for Learning Disability for the 21st Century' to £1.3 million over each of the next three years on advocacy.

Advocates are becoming the new samurai for reducing social and economic disparities. Health advocates help the socially excluded 'gain access to basic health services, training health professionals to deal more competently with minorities, and helping individuals to stand up for themselves.' (Coote 2000 p. 35). They also leap over tall buildings!

Hunt (1998) is absolutely right to suggest that we need increased protection, including relevant legislation to protect advocates against paying excessive personal and economic costs. They should know how hard a journey that is. Probably the very first whistleblower was Sisyphus. He proved that Autolycus was stealing his cattle, pointed the finger and betrayed divine secrets. The Judges of the Dead punished him by the curse of rolling a large block of stone to the brow of a hill and toppling it down the farther slope. He never succeeded in this massive task. After nearly reaching the brow, the weight of the stone pushed him down again over all eternity. So be warned!

REFERENCES

Adam, B D in Moreau, Maurice J (1990) 'Empowerment through Advocacy and Consciousness-Raising: Implications of a Structural Approach to Social Work' *Journal of Sociology and Social Welfare* 17(2)

Advocacy Partners web site – homepages.enterprise.net/horner/ap/apnf/html or their headquarters at 6 Lind Rd, Sutton, Surrey, SM1 4JP

Arnstein, S R (1969) 'A Ladder of Citizen Participation in the USA' *Journal of the American Institute of Planners* 35(4)

Atkinson, D (1999) *Advocacy – a review* Pavilion/Rowntree

Awaaz website: www.comcom.org/awaaz/history.htm

Bahr, H (1973) *Skid Row – an introduction to disaffiliation* Oxford University Press

Barclay Report (1982) *Social Workers – their role and tasks* Bedford Square Press

Bartlett, H (1970) *The Common Base of Social Work Practice* National Association of Social Workers

Bateman, N (1991) 'Legal Lessons' *Social Work Today* 1 August

Bateman, N (1995) 'Advocacy Skills' Arena

Bateman, N (2000) *Advocacy Skills for Health and Social Care Professionals* Jessica Kingsley

Barnes, C (1998) 'Disability, disabled people, advocacy and counselling' in Yvonne Craig (ed.) *Advocacy, Counselling and Mediation in Casework* Jessica Kingsley

Barnes, C, Mercer, G and Shakespeare, T (1999) *Exploring Disability – a sociological introduction* Polity

Begum, N (1992) 'Disabled Women and the Feminist Agenda' *Feminist Review* 40, p. 72

Beresford, P and Croft, C (1993) *Citizen Involvement: a practical guide for Change* MacMillan

Beresford, P (1994) 'Advocacy' in 'Speaking Out for Advocacy - a report of the National Conference' Labyrinth

Biestek, F (1961) *The Casework Relationship* Allen & Unwin

Billis, D (1984) *Welfare Bureaucracies, Their design and change in response to social problems* London Heinemann Educational Books Ltd

Bingley, W and Hurst, R (1987) 'Getting in on the Act' Thames TV

Blakemore, K and Drake, R (1996) *Understanding Equal Opportunities Policies* Harvester Wheatsheaf

Brandon, D and A (1988) *Putting People First – A Handbook on the Practical Application of Ordinary Living Principles* Good Impressions

Brandon, D (1991) *Innovation without Change?* MacMillan

Brandon, D (1994) *The Yin and Yang of Care Planning* Anglia Polytechnic University

Brandon, D with Brandon, A and T (1995) *Advocacy - power to people with a disability* Birmingham Venture Press

Brandon, D (1995) 'Peer Support and Advocacy – international comparisons and developments' in *Empowerment in Community Care* (ed.) Ray Jack Chapman & Hall

Brandon, D and Morris, L (1996) 'Training the Professionals of the Future' *CarePlan* 3(1) September

Brandon, D and Atherton, K (1997) *A Brief History of Social Work* Anglia Polytechnic University

Brandon, S (1997) *'The Invisible Wall' Parents with Attitude*

Brandon, T (1999) Power and disabled People: a comparative case study of three community care services in London Unpublished Ph.D, London School of Economics, June

Brooks, N A (1991) 'Self-Empowerment among Adults with Severe Physical Disability: a case study' *Journal of Sociology and Social Welfare*: 18

Burton, A (1997) 'Dementia: a case for advocacy?' in Hunter, S (ed.) *Research Highlights in Social Work: 31 – Dementia – Challenges and New Directions* Jessica Kingsley

Butler, A and Pritchard, C (1983) *Social Work and Mental Illness* MacMillan

Charity Organisation Society Review (1881) X

Clifford, D J (1995) 'Methods in oral history and social work' *Journal of the Oral History Society* 23(2)

Cohen, D (1988) *Forgotten Millions: the treatment of the mentally ill – a global perspective* Paladin

Coote, A (2000) 'Train health advocates for poor areas' *New Statesman* 18 December

Dalrymple, J and Hough, J (1995) (eds) *Having a Voice – an exploration of Children's Rights and Advocacy* Birmingham, Venture Press

Davies, M (1994) *The Essential Social Worker* Aldershot, Arena

Davis, A and Wainwright, S (1996) 'Poverty Work and the Mental Health Services' *Breakthrough* (1) 1

Department of Health (1999) *National Service Framework for Mental Health* HMSO

Denney, D (1998) *Social Policy and Social Work* Oxford University Press

Dominelli, L (1993) *Social Work: a Mirror of Society or its Conscience?* Sheffield, Department of Sociological Studies

Donnison, D (1991) *Radical Agenda – after the New Right and the Old Left* Rivers Oram Press, p. 63

Dowson, S (1991) 'Keeping it Safe – self advocacy by people with learning difficulties and the response of the services' *Values in to Action*

Ezell, M (1994) 'Advocacy Practice of Social Workers' *Families in Society: The Journal of Contemporary Human Services* January

Flekkoy, M (1989) 'Child Advocacy in Norway: the Ombudsman' *Child Welfare* 68 (2)

Forsyth, B, Melling, J and Adair, R (1996) 'The New Poor Law and conditions in the Pauper lunatic asylum – the Devon experience 1834–1884' *Social History of Medicine* 9 (3)

Francis, R (1991) *Racism and Mental Health – some concerns for social work* National Curriculum Development Project, CCETSW

Freire, P (1982) *Pedagogy of the Oppressed* Penguin

Gathercole, C quoted in Butler, K *et al* (1988) *Citizen Advocacy – a powerful partnership* National Citizen Advocacy

Goffman, E (1961) *Asylums: essays on the situation of mental patients and other inmates* Anchor Books

Goodley, D (2000) *Self-advocacy in the lives of people with learning difficulties* Open University Press

Hadley, R and Clough, R (1996) *Care in Chaos - frustration and challenge in community care* Cassell

Haeuser, A (1976) 'Systematising Advocacy for Anonymous Clients' in Ross, B and Khinduka, S K (eds) *Social Work in Practice* National Association of Social Workers

Hall, J (1997) *Social Devaluation and Special Education - the right to full mainstream inclusion and an honest statement* Jessica Kingsley

Handy, C (1985) *Understanding Organisations* Penguin

Haslam, J (1988) *'Illustrations of Madness' London 1810* – re-published with an introduction by Roy Porter Routledge

Hayden, C, Goddard, J, Gorin, S and van der Spek, N (1999) *State Child Care – looking after children?* Jessica Kingsley

Haynes, K (1996) 'The Future of Political Social Work' in Raffoul, P and McNeice, C A *Future Issues for Social Work Practice* Allyn & Bacon

Holland, M (1991) 'Rights not Rhetoric' *RADAR* (69) p. 10

Hunt, G (ed.) (1998)*Whistleblowing in the Social Services* Arnold

Hunter, R and Macalpine, I (1961) 'John Thomas Perceval (1803-1876) Patient and Reformer' *Medical History* (6)

Jack, R (ed.) (1995) *Empowerment in Community Care* Chapman & Hall

James, A (2000) 'New Mentality' *The Guardian* (26)1 p.6

Jordan, W (1972) *The Social Worker in Family Situations* Routledge & Kegan Paul

Kerr, A and Gregory, E (1998) *The Work of the Guardian Ad Litem* Birmingham, Venture Press

Kohnke, M F (1982) *Advocacy – Risk and Reality* St Louis, The CV Mosby Co

Lancashire Advocacy Development and Support Service (1993) 'Speak Out for Yourself – report of a self advocacy conference in Lancashire'

Leach, B (1996) 'Disabled People and the Equal Opportunities Movement' in Hales, G (ed.) *Beyond Disability – towards an enabling society* Sage

Ledwith, M (1997) *Participating in Transformation* Birmingham,Venture Press

Liberty and BCODP (1994) 'Access Denied: Human Rights and Disabled People' Liberty

Lipsky, M (1980) *Street-Level Bureaucracy. Dilemmas of the Individual in Public Services*, London, Sage

Mayer, J E and Timms, N (1970) *The Client Speaks, working class impressions of casework* Routledge & Kegan Paul

Marshall, T H (1975) *Social Policy* Hutchinson Educational

McDonald, A (1997) *Challenging local authority decisions* Birmingham, Venture Press

Middleton, L (1992) *Children First: working with children and disability* Birmingham, Venture Press

Moody, H. R. (1992) *Ethics in an Aging Society* The John Hopkins University Press

Mondros, J B and Wilson, S M (1994) Organising for power and empowerment. *Empowering the powerless. A Social Work Series* (ed) Gitterman, A New York, Columbria University Press

Monro, J (1758) *Remarks on Dr Batties' Treatise on Madness* London

Morris, J (1993) *Community Care or Independent living?* Joseph Rowntree Foundation

Morris, J (1997) *Community Care: working in partnership with service users* Birmingham, Venture Press

Morris, J (1997) 'Care or Empowerment? A Disability Rights Perspective' *Social Policy & Administration* (31) 1, pp54–60

Munro, J D (1991) 'Training Families in the "Step Approach Model" for effective advocacy' Canada's Mental Health March.

O'Hagan, M (1993) 'Stopovers on my way home from Mars' *Survivors Speak Out*

Oliver, M quoted in Beresford, P and Croft, S (1993) *Citizen Involvement – a practical guide or Change* MacMillan

Oliver, M (1996) *Understanding Disability – from theory to practice* MacMillan

O'Sullivan, T (1999) *Decision Making in Social Work* MacMillan

Parrott, L (1999) *Social Work and Social Care* Gildredge Press

Payne, M (1991) *Modern Social Work Theory: a critical introduction* MacMillan

Perceval, J T (1838 and 1840) *A Narrative of the Treatment Received by a Gentleman, During a State of Mental Derangement* Effingham Wilson

Podvoll, E M (1990) *The Seduction of Madness* Century

Polden, E (1989) 'Social Work and People with Dementia: putting principles into practice' *International Journal of Geriatric Psychology* (4)

Porter, R (1987) *A Social History of Madness* Weidenfeld & Nicolson

PSW (1994)'Civil Rights, society's wrongs: disabled people fight discrimination' *Professional Social Work*

Ramcharan, P (1995) 'Citizen Advocacy and People with learning difficulties in Wales' in Jack, R (ed) *Empowerment in Community Care* Chapman and Hall

Ree, J (1999) *I see a voice - language, deafness and the senses, a philosophical history* Harper/Collins

Rees, S (1978) *Social Work Face to Face* London, Edward Arnold

Robb, B (1967) (ed.) *Sans Everything – a case to answer* Nelson

Robinson, T (1978) *In Worlds Apart* Bedford Square Press

Rogers, A and Pilgrim, D (1993) 'Mental Health and Citizenship' in *Improving Mental Health Practice* CCETSW

Ronstrom, A (1989) 'Sweden's Children's Ombudsman: a spokesperson for Children' *Child Welfare* (68) 2

Rose, J (1994) *Elizabeth Fry – a Biography* MacMillan

Rose, S and Black, B (1985) *Advocacy and Empowerment – Mental Health - care in the community* Routledge & Kegan Paul

Rose, S (1990) 'Advocacy/Empowerment: an approach to clinical practice for Social Work' *Journal of Sociology and Social Welfare* (17)

Sayce, L and Bates, P (2001) 'Disability Rights and Mental Health' *Mental Health Practice*

Schneider, R and Lester, L (2000) *Advocacy in Social Work* Wadsworth

Scott, V (1994) 'Lessons from America - a study of the Americans with Disabilities Act' *RADAR*

Sim, A J and Mackay, R (1997) 'Advocacy in the UK' *Practice* (9) 2

Simon, B in Roberts, R and Nee, R (eds) (1970) *Theories of Social Casework* University of Chicago Press

Simons, K (1993) *Citizen Advocacy – the inside view* Norah Fry Research Centre

Solomon, B B (1976) *Black empowerment: social work in oppressed communities* Columbia University Press

Stern, R (1994) 'Homelessness' *Journal of Interpersonal Care* (8) 2

Stuart, O (1992) 'Double Oppression: an appropriate starting point?' in *The Disabling Society* Open University

Teasdale, K (1998) *Advocacy in Health Care* Blackwell Science

UPIS (1976) *Fundamental Principles of Segregation* Union of the Physically Impaired Against Segregation

United Nations (1971) *Declaration on the Rights of Mentally Retarded Persons* UN, Geneva and New York

United Nations (1994) *Human Rights and Social Work* Centre for Human Rights, UN, Geneva and New York

Waterhouse Enquiry (2000) *Lost in Care* HMSO

Westcott, H and Cross, M (1996) *This Far and No Further: towards ending the abuse of disabled children* Birmingham, Venture Press

Winslade, W *et al.* (1984) 'Making Medical Decisions for the Alzheimer's Patient: Paternalism and Advocacy' *Psychiatric Annals* (14) 3

Wolfensberger, W (1972) *The Principle of Normalisation in Human Services* NIMR

Wolfensberger, W (1977) *A Multi-component advocacy protection schema* Canadian Association for Mental Retardation

Wolfensberger, W (1987) *The new Genocide of Handicapped and Afflicted people* Syracuse University Training Institute

Goldberg Wood, G and Middleton, R R (1991) 'Advocacy and Social Action: Key Elements in the Structural Approach to Direct Practice in Social Work' *Social Work with Groups* (14) pp. 3-4

RELEVANT WEBSITES

Advocacy, Listening and Leverage
> http://dspace.dial.pipex.com/advocacy/text/modelspage.htm

People First
> http://www.peoplefirst.org.uk/pflinks.html

RNIB Information and Advocacy Service
> http://www.rnib.org.uk/ias/address.htm

Promoting Citizen Advocacy in Greater Glasgow
> http://users.colloquium.co.uk/~EQUAL_SAY/home.htm

Citizen advocacy
> http://www.leevalley.co.uk/cait/CitizenAdvocacy.html

Independent Patients Advocacy Service at Rampton Hospital
> *http://dspace.dial.pipex.com/advocacy/V3/*

UKAN
> http://www.comcom.org/acom/ukan.htm